ZEN ON THE TRAIL

Zen on the Trail

HIKING AS PILGRIMAGE

Christopher Ives

Wisdom Publications
199 Elm Street
Somerville, MA 02144 USA
wisdompubs.org

Library of Congress Cataloging-in-Publication Data
Names: Ives, Christopher, 1954– author.
Title: Zen on the trail: hiking as pilgrimage / Christopher Ives.
Description: Somerville, MA: Wisdom Publications, 2018. | Includes
    bibliographical references and index. |
Identifiers: LCCN 2017047782 (print) | LCCN 2017050268 (ebook) |
    ISBN 9781614294603 (ebook) | ISBN 9781614294443 (pbk.: alk. paper)
Subjects: LCSH: Religious life—Buddhism. | Walking—Religious
    aspects—Buddhism.
Classification: LCC BQ5400 (ebook) | LCC BQ5400 .I94 2018 (print) |
    DDC 294.3/4351—dc23
LC record available at https://lccn.loc.gov/2017047782

ISBN 978-1-61429-444-3   ebook ISBN 978-1-61429-460-3

22 21 20 19 18   5 4 3 2 1

Cover design by Marc Whitaker. Interior design by Gopa & Ted2, Inc.
Set in Cardea OTCE 10.5/16. Author photo by Mishy Lesser.

Wisdom Publications' books are printed on acid-free paper and meet
the guidelines for permanence and durability of the Production Guidelines
for Book Longevity of the Council on Library Resources.

♻ This book was produced with environmental mindfulness.
For more information, please visit wisdompubs.org/wisdom-environment.

Printed in the United States of America.

MIX
Paper from
responsible sources
FSC® C005010

Please visit fscus.org.

Contents

Preface

A year before the publication of this book, renowned poet and ecological visionary Gary Snyder generously agreed to offer some words of comment. He crafted a short piece:

> Hiking living
> Standing, sitting, walking, lying. The "Four Dignities."
> Every being with a body learns their life in there.
> The world is before us, and there are people who have walked it all. And then one can do it all just sitting. Knowing that you are truly breathing, and really walking - or sitting - or heck, lie down - makes it a pilgrimage. Gaining being, so that then one can let it go.
> *11. 12. 2017*

I thank Gary for this offering. With his reference to what Zen views as the four main bodily actions, he highlights how Zen extends beyond zazen—seated meditation—to all of our activities, including walking, hiking, living. He also points to how life itself can be lived as a pilgrimage.

I also thank the talented and gracious people at Wisdom Publications who have helped birth this book: Daniel Aitken, publisher; Lindsay D'Andrea, production specialist; Ben Gleason, production editor; Kestrel Slocombe, brand and marketing manager; Dana Guth and Alexandra Makkonen in the marketing department; and Josh

Bartok, executive editor. Josh's superb skills as an editor have made this a much more elegant book than I could ever craft alone.

I am indebted to Len Rosen and Jack LaForte, who read early drafts and provided discerning suggestions, and to hundreds of Stonehill College first-year students who in recent years have joined me in my exploration of pilgrimage in a core course on this practice in relation to religious views of nature.

The backpacking trip described here is a composite of a number of hikes up the Dry River Valley and on Crawford Path, both alone and with others. I thank my wife, Mishy Lesser; my nephew Josh Ives; my cousin Christopher Halsted; and my neighbor David Meshoulam for accompanying me on day hikes and backpacking trips there. I also thank my nephews Ryan Ives, Sam Moss, Max Moss, and Zack Moss for hiking with me on other trails in the White Mountains of northern New Hampshire.

I offer three bows to the Abenaki people, who have cherished those mountains as a sacred home since long before white Europeans—including my ancestors—occupied this land and imposed settler colonialism.

Any mistakes with plant identification or other details are the sole responsibility of the author.

I dedicate this book to Mishy, who with her wise and exuberant love has supported me on all of my journeys, both into the woods of New Hampshire and farther afield. I feel blessed to be walking the trails of life with her at my side.

巡拝

JUNPAI —
"PILGRIMAGE"

Prologue

....

A solitary pilgrim over hills and streams,
wearily rests against his stick.
The steep crags are covered with old moss,
the spring day is long and slumberous.
—SENGAI (1750–1837)[1]

ONE DECEMBER AFTERNOON IN 1998 I rode the Keihan Line back into Kyoto after an outing to Fushimi Inari, a Shintō shrine dedicated to a rice god and famous for the Osaka businessmen who go there each New Year's to drop 10,000-yen notes into the offering box, believing that these equivalents of 100-dollar bills will convince the deity to increase their profits. From the far wall of the train, a poster announced that in a few hours the monks on Mount Hiei would be performing a bonfire ritual for world peace, home safety, good health, and other things for which the faithful might be praying. Ever the fearless scholar of Buddhism, I decided in the moment to head up the mountain and check things out, blissfully disregarding the fact that my only layers were a lightweight shirt and cotton sweater.

I stayed on the train until the Demachi-yanagi terminus. We glided to a halt. The doors whooshed open. I zigzagged around slower riders to the end of the platform and up some steps to the ticket machines for the Keifuku Line, dropped in 450 yen, and snatched the ticket, knowing that the next departure was a minute away—no more, no less, for I was in Japan after all. I jogged through the wicket and boarded the "one-man," a curious appropriation of English that referred less to the solitary conductor in his blue uniform than to the one-car train on which he worked. This rickety senior citizen of the railroad community rattled me through crowded neighborhoods in Kyoto's northeast corner, with views of the Yase River, apron-wearing homemakers on bicycles, and the old capital's few remaining farmhouses, throwbacks sandwiched between drab three-story apartment buildings and gaudy vending machines.

My fellow passengers were nine elderly hikers. Each was bedecked in clunky hiking boots, knee socks, wool knickers, safari shirts, neck towels, canvas hats, and sagging rucksacks.

I briefly wondered which hiker was least likely to make it back down the wooded slopes of the mountain—though hiking on Mount Hiei isn't exactly a Himalayan expedition. After all, the sacred mountain is 26,253 feet lower than Everest. Even so, the graying day-hikers—especially the chalky-faced fellow fidgeting with a pack of Mild Sevens and a disposable lighter—didn't appear to have the stamina that gets cultivated by serious climbers or the renowned ascetics I was heading up the mountain to see.

When we reached Yase, the one-man clanged to a halt. I walked quickly ahead of the booted retirees to get uphill and upwind of the cigarette smoke. Along the path to the cable car station, I passed a diminutive amusement park. Wintering in the shadow of the mountain, the merry-go-round and scrambler wore a gooey patina of mildew. A few steps beyond this bonsai version of Six Flags brought me to the bottom of the cable car.

Ten bucks' worth of yen would get me up near the summit. Surprisingly, the hikers slid thousand-yen notes into the ticket machine, too. Despite all appearances, these elderly folks weren't climbers but descenders.

As the cable car convulsed up an ungodly incline, I thought about my holy destination. On the top of Mount Hiei is Enryakuji, head temple of the Tendai sect of Japanese Buddhism. Renowned Buddhist thinkers like Dōgen (1200–1253) and Nichiren (1222–1282) spent their formative years as acolytes there, until they left and devoted their charisma to founding other Japanese sects.

Enryakuji was established in 788 by the monk Saichō with support from Emperor Kanmu, his patron. Kanmu's relationship with Buddhism was ambivalent at best, for he had led his imperial entourage away from Nara to escape the older Buddhist sects, whose traditional support of the state had morphed into actually trying to take it over. Yet in 803 Kanmu backed a trip to China by Saichō, who returned with Tendai texts and rituals, which Kanmu believed could benefit Heian, his new capital at the foot of Mount Hiei.

Upon his return, Saichō strengthened Enryakuji as the head temple of Tendai in Japan, and in return for supporting these efforts Kanmu obtained religious and political boons: rituals done at the monastery would not only secure the emperor's salvation but ward off unseen dangers. Mount Hiei juts up northeast of Heian, now called Kyoto, and that direction is the "demon's gate" through which evil spirits and misfortune enter Japanese lives. Traditional homes have no doors or windows facing the northeast, similar to how New England saltboxes face south or southeast so their low-sloping back roofs can block cold winds from the northwest. By setting up his capital with a large mountain to the dangerous northeast and capping off this defense with monastics doing protective rituals near the summit, the emperor could keep malevolent spirits from disrupting imperial affairs.

Over the centuries, Enryakuji's job description expanded beyond guard duty. In its prime, the monastery ran pawnshops, extended loans, managed tax-exempt estates, and offered a safe haven to members of the imperial family who had ended up on the losing side of succession battles. The princes who took refuge in its halls became monks, as did others who needed to escape from society. Together with lay monastic workers, many of these renunciates were armed with swords and halberds by their superiors, and whenever the emperor or his officials enacted policies that posed a substantial threat to the interests of the monastery, the abbot would send hordes of these monastic warriors down into the city. They usually shouldered a *mikoshi*, a portable Shintō shrine, enlisting support from the deity temporarily enshrined within it. Once in the capital they would plunk the mikoshi down in a strategic spot until they got their way—a kind of sacred extortion.

For over seven hundred years, Enryakuji was so engaged in political activism like this that in 1571 the warlord Oda Nobunaga, having occupied the capital, dispatched his armies to scramble up the brushy slopes of Mount Hiei and torch the monastery's 3,000 buildings—along with most of the monks inside.

At the end of the cable car line, one glance at the rusted gondola that was waiting to take me the rest of the way up the mountain was enough to pique my interest in a wide trail off to the side. I hiked the rest of the way, about a mile, through tall cedars. The trail delivered me to a parking area below the main buildings of the monastery. The scene there was not what one encounters on the weekend, when the lot is filled with young couples in tinted-window Nissans seeking a romantic spot on a drive. Rather, waiting for me was a cordoned-off area with tables, a roaring bonfire, and a large ritual in full swing. Voicing incantations and moving their hands in symbolic gestures, the priests were burning small slats of wood on which people had written prayers. Central to the esoteric strands of Japanese Buddhism, this *goma* fire ritual consists of an array of chanted mantras, mudras, and, when done inside a temple, mandalas.

But even with its solemnity and roaring flames, the ritual wasn't the main attraction. What pulled me and several thousand Japanese tourist-pilgrims to the upper reaches of the mountain were the officiants. The ritual was being conducted by a squad of monks in formal robes, the most prestigious of whom were "marathon monks," dedicated ascetics who had completed the grueling practice of circumambulating the mountain on circuits as long as fifty miles every day for 100 days, or in some cases for a total of 1,000 days divided into 100- and 200-day chunks over seven years. On each of the days, the monk rises soon after midnight and performs a Buddhist service for an hour. Then, after a simple repast of rice balls and miso soup, he dons white leggings and robes, puts on straw sandals, and sets out on a prescribed course around the flanks of the mountain.[2] As he walks or, more accurately, jogs along the wooded slopes—or on certain days, through Kyoto—he stops at hundreds of shrines, tombs, statues, rocks, trees, springs, and waterfalls, and chants a prayer or mantra at each.

On the far side of the parking lot, our sacred space for the day, the hardened monks, shaded by a striped canopy tent, sipped water or puffed cigarettes. Out in the sun, tourists shopped for amulets, postcards, books about Mount Hiei, incense sticks for their home altars, and prayer slats to be burned by the monks. Food stalls hawked a milky sweet sake called *amazake*, hand-sized rice crackers, and soft drinks. Overlooking the scene was a twenty-foot cement statue of Saichō, about as subtle as the sculptural beast called El Gigante that juts from the rocks at Cinque Terre on the Ligurian coast of Italy. Every hour or so the monks emerged from the tent to repeat the ritual for the next busload of tourists.

A friend in Kyoto once told me about a speech by a marathon monk who had completed the 1,000-day austerity twice, a feat that may never be surpassed. Speaking to college students, Yūsai Sakai made little mention of meditation, attaining high states of consciousness, or communing with nature—none of the stuff that brings most people to the Eastern Religions section of your local bookstore (if you still have one). Rather, he came off as a drill sergeant, telling the students to toughen up, delay gratification, and persevere in their endeavors. Brass-tacks mainstream values or, to the Japanese steeped in them, "common sense."

I had first come to Japan in 1976 with notions that Japan would be exotic, mysterious, and mystical in contrast with the militarized and materialistic culture I had left behind. Back then, on my visits to Mount Hiei and other sacred sites in Japan, I sought things untouched by smog and mini-malls, rarefied, like the hermitages tucked under crags in Sesshū's landscape paintings.

The Japanese stepping off a blue tour bus there in the parking lot seemed untouched by the sublime. They hurried over to the fires, squeezing the ritual into their tight schedules. They paused long enough to take advantage of the photo op and a chance to secure success or better health or a new car by tapping into the power and merit generated by the monks' austerities. Then the uniformed guide with white gloves waved her flag and they scrambled back onto the bus.

Such is snapshot tourism, not limited to that sacred mountain or even Japan. Nibbling at surfaces, in a bubble with tour guides, safe food, and little need to speak with the locals, too many of us choose to travel this way. Around the world, post-modern tourists check sites off the list of the thousand places to see before they die, oblivious of their carbon footprints, nudged onward by advertising blasts like the one that had caught my eye earlier in the day on the limited express from Osaka.

In Japan, this type of tourism encompasses religious traditions that have been commodified for easy consumption, especially now in the midst of an ongoing nostalgia boom. For decades, alienated urban Japanese have been seeking their cultural roots, often on excursions to agrarian hinterlands, marketed by railroads as "returning to one's hometown" (*furusato-gaeri*). Of course, this advertisement of a golden age of communal farming in lush valleys deftly elides the grinding poverty of peasants in past centuries. Ostensibly core components of Japanese culture—rice, sushi, bathing—have a spotty past. Through premodern history most Japanese never ate white rice, never tasted raw tuna on vinegared rice balls with wasabi, and never indulged in nightly soaks in a family tub. Growing rice only to pay oppressive taxes, peasants struggled to survive on rougher grains like millet and sorghum. And their tub was often the closest stream.

As I sat watching the tourists get back on their bus, I realized that evening commitments wouldn't afford me enough time to hike down the mountain. I walked over to one of the stalls and bought an amulet, possibly blessed by Sakai himself. I then headed to a nearby public bus terminus to catch a ride down to Kyoto, the amulet in my pocket giving me a vague sense of security on the cusp of tight curves. I got a window seat and gazed out to the side, diverting my attention from the Japanese on the bus. I felt embarrassed, to no one in particular, for taking the easy way back to the city.

A few minutes down the mountain we passed the graying hikers. They stood in a half-circle at a shrine where a trail cuts across the road. Several of them were wiping their faces with hand towels, while the rest were in prayer, rosaries dangling off their wrists. When the bus swung around the next curve, I looked back over my shoulder, just as they disappeared into the forest, continuing their pilgrimage while I barreled along on the asphalt.

THIS TRIP UP TO ENRYAKUJI GOT ME THINKING about pilgrimage to sacred mountains and how hiking itself can be a form of pilgrimage. It also led me to reflect on the broader question of how to walk on trails or simply be outside in a meditative way, how to deepen one's connection—a lived, conscious connection—to nature.

As a scholar, with that peculiar attachment to defining terms that is typical of my profession, I later crafted a definition of *pilgrimage*. Here it is: "journeying from one's home to a distant sacred site, with encounters and challenges along the way, for the purpose of getting close to something powerful and gaining a benefit, whether a religious experience, peace of mind, healing, a solution to a problem, or even salvation itself." The etymologist in me dug around in *Webster's* and found that the derivation of *pilgrimage* is *peregrinus*, Latin for "foreigner," from *pereger*, "traveling abroad" (as peregrine falcons do), a term that can be further broken down into *per*, "through," and *ager* or *agr*, "land." A pilgrim hence engages in *peregrination*, wandering across the land as a foreigner. One who saunters like this is *sans terre*, without ground or home, and may even end up in *sainte terre*, holy land. Zen might equate this with *fujū* (不住), "no residence" or "nonabiding," when, through nonattachment, we avoid getting stuck and hence can move more freely through life.

In such movement a pilgrim sets out from home to cross the land or an ocean to a distant site believed to be sacred, powerful, or spectacular and hence impactful. Perhaps the place is famous for divine revelations, like Mount Sinai, where a deity called out to Moses through an oddly burning bush and later in the Exodus narrative gave him the "ten utterances," or the Grotto of Massabielle in Lourdes, where the Virgin Mary appeared to Bernadette in 1858. The destination could be a place that elicits a sense of divine presence, such as St. Catherine's Monastery at the foot of the mountain deemed to be Mount Sinai, the Kaaba in Mecca, the Western Wall in Jerusalem, the Ganges in Varanasi, or Mount Wutai in China. Pilgrims may also go to the site of a famous religious experience, like the tree under which the Buddha awakened. Pilgrimages may take believers to places connected to prominent figures in their faith, such as Golgotha inside the Church of the Holy Sepulchre; Santiago de Compostela in northern Spain; the tombs of the patriarchs in Hebron; the Jetavana near Śrāvastī, where the Buddha laid low during rainy seasons; Mount Mercy, where Muhammad gave his last sermon; or the outcropping under the Dome of the Rock in Jerusalem from where Muhammad ascended to heaven on his Night Journey and on which, according to Jews and Christians, Abraham nearly sacrificed his son Isaac.

In Japan, pilgrims head to sacred mountains like Hiei or to Buddhist temples and Shintō shrines that house deities who can confer blessings. One of the most famous Buddhist pilgrimages is to thirty-three temples near Osaka and Nara that are dedicated to Kannon and the thirty-three forms in which she has appeared to help people. Kannon, known in China as Guanyin, is the East Asian version of the bodhisattva Avalokiteshvara, whom Tibetans view as male and believe is incarnated in each of the Dalai Lamas. The two Sino-Japanese characters for *Kannon* connote how she "discerns the sounds" of suffering in the world. This compassionate figure is sometimes represented iconographically with a thousand arms, which are equipped with eyes in the palms of their hands as they radiate outward like peacock plumage. The eyes represent insight into the specific circumstances of anguished beings, while the hands symbolize this bodhisattva's compassionate outreach—her lending a hand—to those beings.

Regardless of the religion, pilgrimage takes the seeker away from daily life. In his classic, *The Ritual Process*, anthropologist Victor Turner describes how rites of passage move through three stages, and his framework applies to pilgrimages as well. The first stage is separation, when the initiate or pilgrim takes leave of society and all the roles, rules, constrictions, and worries. Then, in the second stage of ritual activity, the person enters liminality, from the Latin word *limen*, "threshold" or "border," related to the Greek word *leimōn*, "meadow." In the liminal realm, ordinary life has been bracketed and the person is now either in transition between two social states—as when a male initiate is in an ambiguous zone between boy and man—or simply in a time or place that is set apart from normal life. Once pilgrims have left the structures of ordinary social interactions and entered liminality, they exist in what Turner calls "antistructure." Status distinctions in normal social structures are absent, as pilgrims carry few possessions, wear simple garb, take an attitude of humility, and do the same things as their fellows. This marginal realm is usually austere, calling for abstinence, self-sacrifice, and perseverance through fatigue and pain.[3]

The leveling of people apart from ordinary social life may lead to *communitas,* an ecstatic sense of communion with others, as seen when Lourdes pilgrims walk in the nightly candlelight procession singing the praises of Mary, when two million pilgrims walk from Mecca to the Plain of Arafat, or when Red Sox devotees sing "Sweet Caroline" at Fenway Park. Scholars have recently pointed out that pilgrims, with their differing backgrounds, expectations, and interpretations of the pilgrimage, may not congeal to the extent that Turner claims, but at the very least pilgrims share the belief that their journeys will transform them.

When transformation does occur, it may derive less from the sacred destination than from the time spent in the liminal state, away from ordinary life in society. Carol Winkelmann writes, "The power of pilgrimages extends largely from the experience of liminality—the tenuous, transitory nature of travel, the fleetingness of time, the unfamiliarity or expansion of space, the unmooring of identity from its usual tethers. The travel itself becomes a metaphorical journey of self-realization."[4] The transformation also derives from openness and sustained curiosity. "What matters most on your journey," Phil Cousineau tells us, "is how deeply you see, how attentively you hear, how richly the encounters are felt in your heart and soul."[5] Or as Huston Smith puts it, "openness, attentiveness, and responsiveness are the essence of pilgrimage."[6]

Turner terms the third and final stage of the ritual process "reaggregation." Initiates and pilgrims return to ordinary life in society, changed, with new insights, stories, and status.

Like rites of passage and other forms of ritual practice, traditional pilgrimage is usually grounded in a belief that there is something sacred that exists apart from day-to-day existence, and that we can draw closer to it when we go to power spots, the thin places, or better yet, the thick places, where that higher reality has manifested itself in all of its power in the past and may very well do so again in the present. In their yearning to get close to the sacred, pilgrims typically try to touch something related to it, whether the black stone in the eastern corner of the Kaaba, the walls of the grotto in Lourdes, or the Green Monster in Fenway Park.

Though some pilgrims may think, "I'm going to see where God appeared," in some cases the pilgrim is journeying to be *seen by* divinity. In India, this is *darshan*, about which Diana Eck writes, "The central act of Hindu worship, from the point of view of the layperson, is to stand in the presence of the deity and to behold the image with one's own eyes, to see and be seen by the deity."[7] Apropos of what we just noted about touching, Eck also writes, "In the Indian context, seeing is a kind of touching."[8]

Some pilgrims are trying to *re*connect with the sacred or something that has been lost. This reconnection is a central goal of the spiritual quest if not religion in general. As implied by its derivation, *religare*, "re-link," we can construe "religion" as hooking back onto our source, whether God, the Dao, the Great Spirit, or the natural world. Linguistically, *religion* is kin with a crucial connector on pilgrimage: the ligaments that hold our joints together as we walk.

The longing to reconnect—or simply connect more deeply—with the divine can morph into an intense desire, as seen in the passion of mystics, whose writings abound with imagery of sensual love.

The Song of Solomon includes lines like "Let him kiss me with the kisses of his mouth!" (1:1),[9] "Upon my bed at night, I sought him who my soul loves" (3:1), and "I held him, and would not let him go until I brought him into my mother's house, and into the chamber of her that conceived me" (3:4), which theologians over the centuries have tamed by interpreting them as referring to the soul's communion with God or Christ's love for the Church. But that's the theologians' view—mystics themselves often talk about being the bride of Christ. Granted, for Christians this imagery is metaphorical, not physical, but it does position the mystic in the realm of *eros*, in contrast to *agape*, the unconditional love expressed by Christ.

Despite the disparagement of the body in many religions, including strands of Christianity that are steeped in the Hellenistic split between mind and matter, spirit and flesh, the body is crucial to pilgrimage, and to religious rituals, which are replete with physical imagery, referring not only to kissing and sex but to pain and pleasure, hunger and eating, death and rebirth. Not surprisingly, scholars of ritual have pulled heavily from Freud's theories about how libido, sublimation, repression, and projection play themselves out in dreams, works of art, belief in patriarchal gods, and yes, rituals.

Moving their bodies to sacred sites and contacting higher powers, pilgrims gain benefits. They may get healed, whether in the Ganges at Benares or chilly baths fed by the miraculous spring at Lourdes. They may believe that the pilgrimage will grant them success in a future venture or empower them to help others upon their return to their communities. Their faith may be renewed, and their commitments deepened. They may find acceptance if not forgiveness, whether from Kannon, Mary, Durga, or other caring beings. In this way, they get rejuvenated and renewed—made younger and fresher. Pilgrimage may also help them realize that while they may be in anguish, ultimately it's all okay.

LACING UP BOOTS AND HEADING INTO THE MOUNTAINS, or simply going out for a walk, is, for many of us, a form of pilgrimage. As hikers we take leave of our daily lives: routines, work, stress. We separate from our normal roles and social obligations. We extricate ourselves from strip malls, gas stations, fast food, and technology. We simplify our possessions down to the "ten essentials." As we hike away from the trailhead, we unplug. We go off the grid, away from "civilization." On the trail, in a liminal state, most of our normal social markers have been stripped away as well, for we are all grunting under packs and sweating in similar clothes. Granted, gear freaks with wealth may have snazzier parkas and more bells and whistles on their packs, but we're all peeing under the trees.

Hikers, like pilgrims, are fully embodied. We walk, dirty, with thirst and hunger. Keeping our legs moving, one step at a time, we persevere through blisters, scrapes, sunburn, and sore shoulders. Physical challenges are part of the austerities that hikers share with the religious seekers walking the road from Albuquerque to Chimayo or circumambulating Mount Kailash in Tibet.

But hiking, like pilgrimage, isn't always somber. The pain is leavened with joy. As Gary Snyder reminds us, "The wilderness pilgrim's step-by-step breath-by-breath walk up a trail, into those snowfields [of the high country], carrying all on the back, is so ancient a set of gestures as to bring a profound sense of body-mind joy."[10] Though our bodies ache, our ears are cleansed by the sound of streams whooshing by and wind sighing in the treetops. Our noses savor the smell of pine sap. We feel wonder as we gaze at the Towers of Paine in Patagonia, the sheer cliffs of Yosemite, the massive blocks of ice in the Khumbu Icefall, or the plunging waterfalls of Kauai. And it's not only dramatic spots: we can savor the pleasure of seeing twisted spruce branches above tree line, micro-jungles of moss at the base of old hemlocks, copper lichen presenting itself in quiet glory, and the sedum spreading beside our front steps. We may even find ourselves in ecstasy—from the Greek *ekstasis*, "standing" (*histanai*) "outside" (*ex*)—as we rise up and out of ourselves on summit ridges. When hiking with others, our spirits get lifted by other liminal moments: playing pranks, jumping naked into tarns, sitting in a circle around a fire telling scary stories, piling into tents.

Like the religious pilgrim, on the trail we can connect (or reconnect) with something larger than ourselves, maybe even something we deem sacred. About backpacking and other activities—sailing, kayaking, gardening, peeling garlic, sitting in meditation—Snyder writes, "The point is to make intimate contact with the real world, real self. *Sacred* refers to that which helps take us (not only human beings) out of our little selves into the whole mountains-and-rivers mandala universe."[11]

Then we return. Emerging back at the trailhead, we feel satisfied (ideally), maybe even cleansed. We may feel vividly alive in our sore bodies. An hour later we may find ourselves bombarded by the fluorescent lights in a supermarket as we forage for munchies, and at that point we may realize for the first time how calm and quiet we became on the trail.

Then we cross the threshold back into our homes. Returning to familiars and routines, we may find ourselves feeling more confident, better able to persevere through discomfort and hassles. We may see with greater clarity what really is important. We may discover new gratitude for hot showers and refrigerators, while at the same time missing the simplicity of the trail and the towering hemlock snag halfway up to Asgaard Pass.

WILD NATURE AND MOUNTAINS HAVE ALWAYS CALLED ME. As the son of a scoutmaster and hence a Boy Scout mascot from kindergarten, my imagination was first drawn to nearby Mount Tom and Mohawk Mountain in the Litchfield Hills, then farther up the Berkshires to Bear Mountain in the northwest corner of Connecticut.

After seventeen years of hiking these hills, I moved to the northern terminus of the Berkshires, where as a student in Williamstown I explored Mount Greylock, the Taconics up behind Hopkins Forest, and the Green and White Mountains to the north, linked by the Appalachian Trail as it meanders through New England.

One summer, after helping the Atlantic Cement Company turn quarried limestone into Portland cement at a plant south of Albany, I did my Jack Kerouac imitation, heading out on the road with my thumb and a Greyhound Ameripass. I hiked up beyond the Flat Irons in Boulder while visiting the Naropa Institute in its first summer, scampered up and out of Yosemite Valley into the backcountry, hiked the wilderness beach strip on the west side of the Olympics, and traversed alpine meadows above Banff.

After college I headed to Japan and explored other heights at Myōshinji, one of the head temples of the Rinzai Zen sect. During my year outside Osaka and four years in Kyoto, I bushwhacked the tangled slopes of Dog Cry Mountain (Inunaki-*san*) in the Izumi range and Mount Hiei out behind my hillside flat in Kyoto. My motorcycle took me to Kurama down on the Kii Peninsula, Mount Hira in Shiga, Daisetsuzan volcano in Hokkaidō, and trailheads below Tateyama and other peaks in the Japan Alps.

Zen study led me to join a mentor, Buddhist philosopher Masao Abe, in Claremont, east of L.A., up against the San Gabriel Mountains. Six years in grad school there afforded hikes up Mount Baldy and San Gorgonio, and jaunts to Joshua Tree, Death Valley, the Sierras, and beyond. In 1983 I took a semester off and headed to the Himalayas. A flight from Kathmandu to Lukla on a STOL plane— "short takeoff and landing"—set me up for a trek up through Solu-Khumbu. I hiked past the mega-Matterhorn glory of Ama Dablam and up Kala Patar to get an unobstructed view of the pyramidal crown of Everest, the sheer north face of Nuptse, and the Everest base camp at the foot of the terrifying Khumbu Icefall.

Even after mountains of that scale, the Cascades held my curiosity and awe for fourteen years after I moved from Claremont to Tacoma for a teaching position at the University of Puget Sound and frequent hikes and backpacking trips. I feasted on the glaciated slopes of Rainier and Baker, the vertical thrust of Boston Peak, the alpine landscape above Asgaard Pass in the Enchantments, and the old-growth rainforests below Mount Olympus, Anderson Pass, and Upper Lena Lake. And on a journey to Europe that I tucked in between research trips to Asia, I traipsed among the Alps.

Now back in New England for the past fourteen years, with crackly knees and sore back, I hike in the White Mountains or head out west from time to time to the Maroon Bells, Mount Edith Cavell, the slot canyons of Escalante, or the cliffs of Zion.

THIS BOOK IS A REFLECTION ON HIKING AS A FORM OF PILGRIMAGE, especially in relation to Buddhist religious endeavors in the mountains. It is also an attempt to put into words some of the inklings and practices that have emerged on my trips into "the woods." I hope to sketch a particular way of being in nature, or more exactly, a way of *being* nature, as well as a way of integrating the fruits of the trail back into our ordinary lives. Though my main focus is on the spirituality of hiking, I offer this book in the hope that it can help us realize our embeddedness in nature and, ultimately, realize ourselves *as* nature, expressing itself in the shifting form that is our mind/body, as we hike in the Alaskan wilderness, walk down the street in Boston, or travel along other stretches of our lifelong pilgrimages in this vast and beautiful world.

ONE

Leaving Home

出家

SHUKKE —
"RENUNCIATION"

One departs the home to embark on a quest into an archetypal wilderness that is dangerous, threatening, and full of beasts and hostile aliens. This sort of encounter with the other—both the inner and the outer—requires giving up comfort and safety, accepting cold and hunger, and being willing to eat anything. You may never see home again. Loneliness is your bread. Your bones may turn up someday in some riverbank mud.

—GARY SNYDER[12]

THE FIRST CHIRPING lifts me out of a dream about shaking my hands to shoo evil spirits off a ledge. I throw back the sheet and swing my legs off the bed. My lower back seizes up as I stand, then, just as abruptly, releases. As I fill the kettle, I glance out at the maple branches above our patchy moss garden and realize that for the first time in five days the sun is rising into a blue sky. Then the tug: up in New Hampshire, the Dry River is tumbling down from Oakes Gulf on the south side of Mount Washington, luring me out of Boston.

In the attic I take gear off a rickety metal bookcase. In more frenetic moments I toss stuff into a bag and head to the trail, or the gym, or a friend's place for the night, but today I try to take it slow so I can contain the adrenaline flowing expectantly into my quads. I lay the items on an oriental rug that was once in my Tacoma living room and is now relegated, together with my old black leather recliner, to a dusty existence under the trusses. Though not as valuable as the "simple" bowls, caddies, ladles, and whisks in *cha-no-yu*, I try to handle all my equipment with at least a smidgeon of the attentiveness of an Urasenke tea master choosing the utensils and bowls that fit the season or the day's weather. Though I like to think of myself as someone with few attachments, my gear is precious to me and I take care of it, for it has been my companion on many a hike and I'm well aware of its role in my comfort and possibly my survival once I get up the trail. As backcountry first-aid instructors will tell you, when it comes to first aid, "wilderness" begins one mile up the trail or thirty minutes from the back of an ambulance. That fact echoes in the back of my mind as I assemble the items I'll need for the day.

Water bottle. Daypack. Mesh bag with headlamp, bug repellent, waterproof matches, iodine tablets, toilet paper, whistle. Compact first-aid kit. Swiss army knife—the thing Aron Ralston left behind when he ventured into that slot canyon in Utah. Red Sox cap. Sunblock. Crinkled topo map of southern Presidentials. Compass. Fleece jacket. Bic lighter in baggie to carry in the zipper pocket on my shorts (which gets me wondering . . . how often is it that hikers lose their packs in the woods, or in a river, and then need to start a fire to survive?). Wool cap and light polypro gloves with a hole in one fingertip from touching the wrong log in a campfire last summer. Sunglasses. Wicking T-shirt. Nylon cargo shorts. Gore-Tex shell. Bandana. Lip balm. Gaiters. Trekking poles. Hiking boots glistening with the waterproofing goo I smeared on after my last outing. Low-cut hiking shoes, in case the trail has started drying out.

Then I feel a tug to extend my jaunt into a two-day backpacking trip. I grab my Osprey pack, bug bivy, sleeping bag, and small pad. From a cardboard box I take my cooking and eating gear: stove, canister of propane, titanium spork, Sierra cup, and one-quart pot with lid. Recalling how the trees around my likely tent site offer few big branches out to their sides, and by extension how long it took last time to rig avalanche cord to hang my food bag, I also grab the bear canister.

As I do this, I recall the refrain chanted by engineers at the Japanese company I translated for in graduate school: *dandori hachibu*, "preparation is 80 percent." This maxim echoes another piece of Japanese advice, which I fail to follow each time I walk up to a buffet table: *hara hachibu*, "gut eight parts," which connotes eating until you're feeling 80 percent full and then stopping to allow physical satiation to catch up with your mental craving and busy chopsticks.

I lay each piece of gear out on the rug. I check to make sure the batteries in the headlamp are strong, the lighter works, and there's enough toilet paper. Then I put the small stuff in a plastic milk crate and haul everything downstairs. In the kitchen I grab an apple, a bagel, a chunk of pecorino, two packets of instant oatmeal, and two ramens. I take two ziplock bags out of a drawer and into one I spoon some instant coffee and in the other I mix peanut M&Ms, almonds, and raisins. For the car ride home, I also mix up a bag of salty-crunchy snacks: rice crackers, peanuts, Cajun sesame sticks, and giant corn nuts.

Like a hiker, when an aspiring Zen monk performs his act of renunciation, termed *shukke*, literally, "leaving home,"[13] he packs a prescribed set of possessions. Traditionally, he's a male in his teens, and after the first step of ordination—"receiving" the ten moral precepts from a local temple priest, often his own father—he performs *angya*, "going on foot" to the place where he'll train. "When setting out for a monastery," Zen master Sōkō Morinaga tells us, "you take a *bunko*, a satchel-sized box that contains your monastic robe. A pair of bundles hung from your shoulders holds your other possessions: eating bowls, chopsticks, a whetstone and razor for shaving, sutra books, undergarments, and a raincape. You wear the traditional outfit of leggings, straw sandals, and wicker hat, tucking up the robe with a band."[14]

Once a Zen monk is accepted at a monastery, he'll be provided with the traditional "four requisites": food, clothing, shelter, and medicine, or as early Buddhist texts put it, alms, rags, a tree, and urine. (I don't know why urine was seen as medicinal, but luckily for contemporary monks, Buddhist medical savvy has improved in the intervening millennia.) In Theravadan Buddhist monasteries a monk's possessions are typically restricted to three robes, a belt, a razor, a needle, a begging bowl, and a filter for straining living organisms out of drinking water.[15]

Feeling a bit monkish, I try to reduce my gear to the bare necessities. Minimal weight, minimal volume—stripping away, but making sure I have the ten essentials. If only my sixty-year-old brain could remember what they are. Let's see. Rain gear, fire-starting materials, map and compass, headlamp, water, extra food, extra layers, first-aid kit . . . and then my mind goes blank. What the heck are nine and ten? Oh yeah, some sort of shelter, like a bivy sack. And the tenth . . . was it protection from the sun? Sounds right. Sunblock, hat, sunglasses. And for good measure, the eleventh essential: actually knowing how to use the compass.

It's June, with a decent forecast, so I set aside my 200-weight fleece jacket. But I grab a quarter-zip pullover and keep the wool hat and polypro gloves in the mix. Though I'm packing for an overnight trip, I hear echoes of my day-hike mantra: "Hike light, but have the gear needed for two nights in the woods with a broken ankle." Unlike mendicants and pilgrims who rely on the alms and logistical support offered by people along the way, hikers may have to depend on themselves.

And what gadgets to bring? That's simple for me—I have no satellite phone or GPS unit, which renders me little different from Paleolithic hunters, though I haven't been quite able to give up my Gore-Tex for deerskin. Today my electronics will be a headlamp and watch. And just in case, my cell phone. Not that I'll be able to use it once I get up into the Dry River drainage, but I've heard something about how it can emit a ping even where there's no reception—a definite plus for solo hikers.

Though we call it backpacking, we could just as easily call it home-packing, or home-carrying. It's a powerful expression of simplicity: carrying everything we need—food, clothing, shelter, medical supplies, water—on our backs. Someday I want to empty a backpack next to the contents of an average American home.

As if putting my favorite cups and glasses in a box on moving day, I stow the items carefully in the pack. I start by inserting the minimalist sleeping pad, and into the tube it forms I place the bear canister, and into it I place most of the food, the stove, and the pot, which in turn contains my wool cap and gloves. Next I pack the gas canister, cup, fleece layer, shell, ditty bag with odds and ends, and baseball cap. In the top pouch I place the sunblock, map, compass, and plastic bag for trash. In the bottom compartment I stuff the sleeping bag and bug bivy. Finally, to the outside of the pack I strap two trekking poles, anticipating the jabs in my knees when I scamper down Crawford Path at the end of the hike. I fill a water bottle and put it next to the bag of gorp; at the trailhead I'll slide them into outside pouches on the pack. I check the laces on my hiking boots as I set them by the door. Into one boot I stuff a pair of Smartwool socks, which seem to work better than my dumbwool pair. And in the other boot I place a jar of petroleum jelly to smear inside my thighs at the trailhead to prevent chafing.

Each time I do this packing ritual it settles me. My senses are right there with the gear. The checking and packing of the essentials draw my attention away from the unread email messages on my laptop and the to-do list on my desk. As I pour myself into this preparation, the anxiety that pervades so many of my days begins to dissipate.

After a quick breakfast of oatmeal and coffee, I tell my wife, Mishy, where I'm going and my expected time of return. I give her a lingering kiss. I pick up the pack and boots, reach for the keys, and head out to my Impreza. As I unlock the car, I bow slightly at the house to mark my shukke, my renunciation of the comfort of home. Like Turner's pilgrims, it's time to separate from my ordinary life. My departure is consecrated by the sun pouring in through the windshield and maple leaves dancing in a light breeze as I drive away on Oliver Street.

TWO

The Threshold: Temple Gate and Mountain Trailhead

山門

SANMON —
"MOUNTAIN GATE"

Thus says the Lord: Stand at the crossroads, and look,

and ask for the ancient paths, where the good way lies;

and walk in it, and find rest for your souls.

—JEREMIAH 6:16

Unlike people, who are constantly trying to make things happen,

the trail receives whatever comes. It rejects nothing, nor does it

judge, or choose, or lament what it gets. It represents the "meek"

of the Beatitudes, and the trail is indeed a beneficiary of an inheri-

tance that it is willing to share. The trail and its surrounding forest

are rich beyond any human concept of wealth.

—STEPHEN ALTSCHULER[16]

THREE HOURS LATER, after stopping on Bear Notch Road to look north at the Presidentials and the Dry River Valley extending up to the base of Oakes Gulf, I pull over in the grass on the side of Route 302 at the trailhead, just south of Crawford Notch. The temperature has already risen to seventy, and judging from the sticky air, I sense that the dew point is hovering around there, too.

I slip my feet into the Smartwool socks. Seeing how wet the woods are, I leave my hiking shoes in the trunk and grab my scarred Vasque boots. I pull them on. I draw the laces tight and double-knot them. I put on the gaiters, and spray Deet bug juice on my exposed knees, arms, and neck. I wonder whether the permethrin I sprayed on the socks and shorts the other day will help repel ticks. I insert the water bottle into the mesh pocket on the side of my pack, put the gorp in the top pocket, and spread sunblock on my face and SPF 30 balm across my lips. I roll a bandana, lay it across my forehead, and tie it in back. I put on my sunglasses, with the retainer looped behind my neck. I turn off my cell phone. I lock the car and zip my keys, wallet, and cell phone into the top pouch of the pack.

For years I have done similar rituals when entering *zendōs*, Zen meditation halls, including the small room in our attic that the previous owner walled out for bluegrass guitar picking. When I enter that room, I bow once. Palms still together before my chest, eyes turned down, I walk slowly, feeling the rug beneath my feet. I stop in front of my cushions: a round *zafu* resting on top of a square *zabuton*. As I sit down, the zafu feels firm beneath me. I pick up a stick of Mainichikō incense and light one end with a Bic lighter. I set the other end into the hole in the shell I use as a holder and, with a wave of my hand, extinguish the tiny flame. Sitting erect, I put my hands into a meditation position, lower my gaze to the rug, and pour myself into a long outbreath, the first step to quieting my mind and opening up the calm attentiveness that some call "mindfulness." Like many practitioners of Buddhism in the West, I tend to construe mindfulness as paying attention. Though this is one connotation of the Pali term *sati*, in many texts this term means "recollecting," so to translate it the Chinese used the character *nien* (念), "to recollect or remember," which consists of two parts, "now" (今) and "mind" (心).

At the trailhead, mindfulness as both attentiveness and recollection comes into full play. Do I have all the gear that I need? Are all of the pockets and compartments of my pack zipped closed? Rock climbers do the same sort of thing. Is my climbing harness on properly? Am I roped up correctly? Do I know what I'm doing?

I lift the pack and slide my left arm under the shoulder strap, hoisting the twenty-odd pounds onto my trapezius muscle, then extend my right arm under the other strap to get the pack all the way up on my back. I take the two ends of the hip belt and clip the buckle together. I pull down on the ends of the shoulder straps and the load-lifter straps. I clip the sternum strap together. My attention is sharpened by the crisp sound of the buckle clipping—a hiker's bell of mindfulness. I complete this ritual by pulling the stabilizer straps on either side of the hip belt. With everything tightened and fastened, the pack should move with me as an appendage of my body, not flopping or sagging, even though my body has started flopping and sagging in recent years.

In the corner of many trailhead parking lots stands the information board, with a rough topo map, litter admonitions, tick drawing, and bear warning. The wooden structure, usually two four-by-fours, a plywood backing, and a cedar shingled roof, reminds me of a *mon*, a temple gate, the threshold—Turner's *limen*—through which one must pass to enter the realm of Zen practice. When an aspiring monk goes to a monastery, the first act is to pass through the "mountain gate" (*sanmon*) into the expanse of the temple complex, which includes the monastery proper: the monks' hall (*sōdō*). The character for *mon* can also mean "teachings," which are studied once one has walked through the gate and into sacred monastic space. The gate is the portal to awakening, to truth. Jesus said, "I am the gate. Whoever enters by me will be saved, and will come in and go out and find pasture" (John 10:9). We are also told that "the gate is narrow and the road is hard that leads to life, and there are few who find it" (Matthew 7:14). Zen thresholds are tight, so much so that a master once proclaimed, in grand Zen fashion, "There is no gate into the Great Way" (*daidō mumon*). This notion lies behind the title of one of the most important collections of koans, *The Gateless Barrier*,[17] with the ideograph for *barrier* referring to border stations between regions, whether on a mountain pass or a valley road.

When he gets to the monks' hall, the aspirant encounters another threshold. Traditionally, for several days he has to kneel at the entrance in supplication. This is called *niwa zume*, "stuck in the garden." At night he is allowed to enter for a few hours of sleep in a cramped guest room, but before reclining he must sit in meditation a while longer. The next morning he has to go back outside and continue crouching.

Should he persevere through two days of this, he is permitted to come inside for good. But the ordeal isn't over. He is led to a room where he is stuck once again, in meditation, for five more painful days. He is given only water and gruel. This is *tanga zume*, literally, "stuck beyond dawn," but translated by Zen master Eishin Nishimura as "examination in the guest room."[18] Monks will observe the supplicant's perseverance as his legs start to scream. He is stuck at the final threshold, waiting to cross over into the space beyond: the meditation hall in which the monks live. Like a Lakota boy enduring the intense heat of the sweat lodge, then fasting and sitting alone up in the hills for four days in his quest for a vision, the Zen seeker must endure the pain of his tradition's choosing.

At the trailhead for the Dry River Trail, it's time for me to pass through today's gate into the backcountry. Here is where I do a second separation, leaving roads and machines behind. This is also a moment of entering, for I now venture into my sacred space, my sacred time.

At this threshold I pause to put my palms together and bow goodbye to my car and the realm of roads, buildings, and computers. I wonder if anyone is watching me and glance self-consciously up and down Route 302 to my left and right. I feel like Janus, the Roman guardian of gates, with his two faces, watching over beginnings, including the beginning of the year, in the month named for him.

Then I turn 180 degrees and, as if bowing my way into a zendō, prostrating in the direction of the Kaaba, or genuflecting in church,

I lower my head to the woods. I try to show humility, respect, and gratitude—and appreciate being able to do so without the pain of someone "stuck in the garden." I do this to remind myself, to be mindful, that I am crossing a boundary into a place that demands and deserves my attention. For me it is a sacred space, not in the sense of a realm of spirits and gods—who knows, they may indeed reside in the thickets and cliffs up the trail—but as a place to let go of worries, reactions, comparisons, and other uninvited guests that refuse to leave the interior home that is my mind.

With the bow I let the woods know that I'm entering, as if asking permission. I listen. A robin calls out to its mate in a nearby oak, and somewhere up the road in the direction of Crawford Notch a couple of crows are squawking.

Thirty feet in I encounter the information board for this trail. Posted on it is a laminated map of the Dry River drainage and posters about bear encounters, "leave no trace" camping, and trail restoration work in the wake of Hurricane Irene four years ago.

Though these woods were once logged and one section of the trail follows an abandoned rail bed, I am entering a place that feels wild. It's even designated as a wilderness area. Certainly not as vast as the backcountry of Yellowstone, but at least free from pavement and subdivisions, and from the groomed New England landscape surrounding barns that house cows or, more likely nowadays, horses belonging to wealthy equestrians from New York. I can lose myself in the sedums, moss, and rocks in our garden, and I can find wildness in Watertown, but I often long for wilderness as defined by the Wilderness Act of 1964: "a wilderness, in contrast with those areas where man and his own works dominate the landscape, is hereby recognized as an area where the earth and its community of life are untrammeled by man, where man himself is a visitor who does not remain."[19] (Though of course, this definition does not recognize that for millennia native peoples "remained" in what modern urbanites have labeled "wilderness.") Knowing the scale of nature on the East Coast, I calibrate my desires and rest content with places that at least have some woods, streams, and hills, ideally with few roads and minimal human habitation.

Over my initial five years in Japan, the tug to get into the woods never left me. Whenever people asked me how I liked living there, I always talked about how intrigued I was by Japan—the individual people, the art, the religious traditions—but with one caveat: almost as if I were reading from a script, I would add that I longed for "wide-open spaces," for woods and trails that were not clogged with other hikers. That being said, I did learn to love nature the way the Japanese do: I took note of the changing seasons; I went to see cherry blossoms each spring; I spent many a fall day relishing the maple foliage at Manshūin Temple on the edge of my neighborhood in northeast Kyoto. But the Japanese "love of nature" is not without controversy.

D. T. Suzuki, widely known communicator of this love to English speakers, once argued that "Zen's habit of mind, to break through all forms of human artificiality and take firm hold of what lies behind them, has helped the Japanese not to forget the soil but to be always friendly with Nature and appreciate her unaffected simplicity."[20] In a discussion of mountaineering he makes related claims:

> The idea of the so-called "conquest of nature" comes from Hellenism, I imagine, in which the earth is made to be man's servant, and the winds and the sea are to obey him. Hebraism concurs with this view, too. In the East, however, this idea of subjecting nature to the commands or service of man according to his selfish desires has never been cherished. . . . Yes, we climb Fuji, too, but the purpose is not to "conquer" it, but to be impressed with its beauty, grandeur, and aloofness; it is also to worship a sublime

morning sun rising gorgeously from behind the multicolored clouds.[21]

Even before I read Edward Said's *Orientalism*, I wondered about this East-West binary. And early on in my initial stay in Japan, as my study of Japanese became more obsessive—with vocab flash cards nestled beside the toilet in Izumisano, as my apartment mate and co-teacher Damian still reminds me—I discovered that the Japanese term closest to "nature" is *shizen*, a two-character compound literally meaning "self-so," which is to say "in the manner of itself." This expression was imported from China, where the compound is pronounced *ziran*. It appears in such texts as the *Daodejing* and the *Zhuangzi*, connoting the way things express themselves in accordance with their natures, how they unfold when left undisturbed, and how people act when they drop all effort and artifice. Carrying this connotation, *shizen* is roughly equivalent to "spontaneously," as indicated in a third-century commentary on the *Zhuangzi*: "What is spontaneously so, and not made to be so, is the natural. The roc can fly in high places, the quail in low ones. The *da'chun* tree can live for a long time, the mushroom for a short time. All of these capacities are natural, and are not caused or learned."[22]

In Zen, *shizen* also designates the spontaneous freedom that emerges when we break beyond the constricted ego and act without conscious reflection. This was emphasized—and misconstrued—by Kerouac, Ginsberg, and other Beats who sought "Zen" freedom without having to undergo the monastic training on which true freedom is based.[23] Their message was to stop being uptight and "square," to loosen up. Not bad advice—but not exactly Zen either.

In modern Japanese, as the term closest in connotation to the English word "nature," *shizen* also refers to the natural realm: the world of mountains, spring flowers, and autumn leaves that permeate Japanese arts. Shizen holds center stage in Shintō with its animistic reverence of distinctive natural objects and forces that it regards as *kami*. Back in the eighteenth century, Motoori Norinaga wrote, "In ancient usage, anything whatsoever that was outside the ordinary, possessed superior power, or was awe inspiring was called *kami*."[24] As proclaimed in the cosmogony of the *Kojiki* myth and demarcated on the landscape by Shintō shrines, kami in many cases are—or simply reside in—natural features that are distinctive, such as Mount Fuji or the Nachi waterfall. Japanese have believed that these deities exist across the archipelago, and as a result they have also believed that Japan is *shinkoku*, "the land of the kami," or, as ultranationalists have preferred to translate it, "the divine country."

In the Japanese aesthetic tradition, however, the nature that is most appreciated is not wild or grand. The Ryōanji rock garden in Kyoto, carefully pruned bonsai trees, the arrangement of a single flower for the tea ceremony, and Bashō's epigrammatic haiku poems are said to epitomize the Japanese love of nature. As indicated by these exemplars, though, it is shaped and miniaturized nature that the Japanese have loved the most. In this way of loving nature, as long as one has a twig, one does not need the forest.

This is stylized, not wild, nature. This is not the musky realm of rotting nurse logs, mud, and mosquitoes in the Olympic rainforest; nor the wind and slashing rain of a typhoon; nor the fire that is essential to the sustenance of Douglas fir stands; nor the sweat and blood of childbirth. In fact, blood, one of the key reminders that we are embodied creatures with natural rhythms in concert with the moon, has been looked on as a defiling impurity since the earliest times in Japan, as has death, the full transformation of our physical existence back into the larger natural cycles that sustain all life. Because of blood taboos, some of the most spectacular mountains of Japan, designated as sacred, were off-limits to women. Similarly, because of the association of Buddhist priests with death and funerals, you will never see a Buddhist cleric wearing robes in a Japanese hospital. And as I learned in my first year in Japan, a bundle of incense sticks, though cool in the 1960s here in Massachusetts, is not the most romantic souvenir to bring back from a day of visiting temples and give to the Japanese woman you have just started dating: given the strong association between incense and Buddhist rituals for the dead, I might as well have brought her a skull.

Gary Snyder calls *shizen* "a bland and general word,"[25] arguing in its stead for "wild" (in Japanese, *ya*). "Wild" includes *shizen* by connoting "flourishing in accord with innate qualities" but goes beyond it by also implying "natural excess and exuberance"; "unintimidated, self-reliant, and independent" people; and behavior that is "outrageous, 'bad,' admirable . . . artless, free, spontaneous, unconditioned" and "expressive, physical, openly sexual, ecstatic."[26] Ironically, the very thing for which I just criticized Kerouac and Ginsberg—taking Zen naturalness and "spontaneity" to be a sensual, iconoclastic wildness rather than the kind of spontaneity that emerges from years of training—might hold more promise as a resource for ecological living than "authentic" Zen does.

This is not to say that wild nature is totally negated by Japanese religions. Less tamed places in nature—especially mountains—are seen as sites of power, and for centuries ascetics like the marathon monks have been venturing into rugged areas to tap that power through austerities and then use it to help people in need. But their focus is on particular spots seen as powerful, whereas Snyder's focus is on broader wilderness, as "a *place* where the wild potential is fully expressed, a diversity of living and nonliving beings flourishing according to their own sorts of order,"[27] a place that is "richly interconnected, interdependent, and incredibly complex."[28] This is nature as it bursts forth in and around us in a wild profusion of flesh, blood, roots, rocks, and waves, free from human attempts to harvest, shrink, or refine it. And in some cases nature manifests itself in "irrational, moldy, cruel, parasitic"[29] forms that have never been invited into Japanese teahouses.

Japanese are not alone in preferring tamed nature. In the "pure lands" depicted in Indian and Chinese Buddhist texts, trees and flowers are made out of jewels, and there are no animals except birds, whose melody pleases the humans reborn there.[30] According to historian Peter Coates, in the Western imagination, "If rugged places were bracketed with hell, gardens were invested with heavenly qualities. Medieval conceptions of paradise, both earthly and celestial, fed off various established traditions of affection not only for gardens, shady groves and other pastoral locales but also for hunting reserves: the term 'paradise' (*pairidaëza*), whose literal meaning is 'walled enclosure,' was originally used for the Persian nobility's hunting parks."[31]

Stepping off the *Mayflower*, William Bradford saw "a hidious & desolate wilderness, full of wild beasts & willd men."[32] He and other early Europeans in North America viewed wilderness as a chaotic, dangerous realm of Satan, a place where good people lose control of their sinful impulses. *Wilderness* derives from *wild-dēor-ness*, a place inhabited by wild beasts,[33] and to the Puritans, "Wilderness was, literally, the place of wild beasts: the fear was that, in the primitive forests with the beasts, one would become confused, bewildered, losing a sense of self and society that was essential to civilized life and to salvation thereafter."[34] In their westward push, settlers brought along these beliefs about wild areas and the "savages" who had resided there for millennia.

Even Thoreau, when venturing out from pastoral Concord, could get bewildered by wilder places. As he describes in *The Maine Woods* (1864), while climbing up the summit ridge of Mount Katahdin through "savage and dreary scenery"[35] he discovers that some part of the beholder, even some vital part, seems to escape through the loose grating of his ribs as he ascends. He is more lone than you can imagine. There is less of substantial thought and fair understanding in him, than in the plains where men inhabit. . . . Vast, Titanic, inhuman Nature has got him at disadvantage, caught him alone, and pilfers him of some of his divine faculty. She does not smile on him as in the plains. She seems to say sternly, why came ye here before your time? . . . I cannot pity nor fondle thee here, but forever relentlessly drive thee hence to where I *am* kind."[36]

Unlike the Puritans, however, Thoreau knew the value of the wild. In "Walking" he penned the oft-quoted line, "In Wildness is the preservation of the World,"[37] and in *Walden* he wrote, "We can never have enough of Nature. We must be refreshed by the sight of inexhaustible vigor, vast and Titanic features, the sea-coast with its wrecks, the wilderness with its living and its decaying trees, the thundercloud, and the rain which lasts three weeks and produces freshets. We need to witness our own limits transgressed, and some life pasturing freely where we never wander."[38]

With these comments Thoreau was on the vanguard of the shift away from Puritan moralistic views of wild nature, a shift that was promoted in large part by John Muir. Following the Civil War, Muir roamed the mountains of California, started the Sierra Club, and advocated for the creation of national parks. He offered advice to his fellow Americans: "Climb the mountains and get their good tidings. Nature's peace will flow into you as sunshine flows into trees. The winds will blow their freshness into you, and the storms their energy, while cares will drop off you like falling leaves."[39] Issuing this call, Muir helped facilitate something new: "After the psychologically important 'ending' of the American frontier in 1890, the scarcity theory of value began to work on behalf of wilderness. Americans were becoming civilized enough to appreciate wilderness. They could begin to understand it as an asset, not an adversary."[40]

Since then many of us have yearned for "pristine wilderness." This desire, like most desires, has not been without consequences for others. When the first national parks were carved out in the late 1800s and early 1900s, the government, in an attempt to protect supposedly untrammeled areas, removed indigenous people from what we know now as Yosemite, Yellowstone, and Glacier National Parks. They had been living there for over 10,000 years, with no notion of "nature" or a "wilderness" separate from their place of hunting, gathering, sleeping, and storytelling. And then they were dispossessed.[41]

At present, national parks do provide sanctuaries for many of us, and there is good reason to cherish them. But our cherishing needs to extend beyond the magnificent, the powerful, the supposedly pristine. To revere remote wilderness and set aside only certain spots as protected or sacred can make it easier to trash the not-so-wild that is closer to home. As Gary Snyder writes about Japan,

> Even in the midst of the onrushing industrial energy of the current system, shrine lands still remain untouchable. It would make your hair stand on end to see how a Japanese developer will take bulldozers to a nice slope of old pines and level it for a new town. When the New Island was created in Kobe harbor to make Kobe the second busiest port in the world (after Rotterdam), it was raised from the bay bottom with dirt obtained by shaving down a whole range of hills ten miles south of the city. This was barged to the site for twelve years—a steady stream of barges carrying dirt off giant conveyor belts that totally removed soil two rows back from the coast. The newly leveled area became

a housing development. In industrial Japan it's not that "nothing is sacred," it's that the *sacred* is sacred and that's *all* that's sacred.[42]

Now in the twenty-first century, with nature lovers buying gear at REI, reading *Outside* magazine, and looking for adventure, wilderness areas are getting loved to death. The solitude that draws us into the woods is getting harder to find, and as I start walking away from Route 302, I hope, selfishly, that no one else will be hiking up the Dry River Valley today.

THREE

Breath and Body

TAIGEN —
"EMBODIMENT"

....

> Walking, ideally, is a state in which the mind, the
> body, and the world are aligned, as though there
> were three characters finally in conversation
> together, three notes suddenly making a chord.
> —REBECCA SOLNIT[43]

> The universe is composed of subjects to be communed with,
> not objects to be exploited. Everything has its own voice.
> —THOMAS BERRY[44]

> Ask the animals, and they will teach you;
> the birds of the air and they will tell you;
> ask the plants of the earth, and they will teach you;
> and the fish of the sea will declare to you.
> —JOB 12:7–8

ABOUT A HALF-MILE FROM THE TRAILHEAD, walking under oaks on the west side of the river, I realize that since I left the car I've been obsessing about how to defend the liberal arts in the face of narrowly vocational approaches to higher education. Long ago Yunmen (864-949) purportedly admonished his disciples: "If you sit, just sit; if you walk, just walk—but don't wobble." When I hike, I try to focus on each breath, and each step, one at a time. If I notice that I'm worrying about work or daydreaming about something back home, I bring my attention back to what I'm doing with my body. Just this breath, just this step. I twist fewer ankles this way. Thoreau wrote that his reason for retreating to a cabin in the woods beside Walden Pond was to "live deliberately." When I set out on the trail, I try to hike deliberately.

Of course, this is easier said than done. It's hard not to be scattered, especially in lives that are way too busy. Some of us may even wear our scurrying as a badge, as if it indicates that we're important, doing impactful cutting-edge things in the world. When busyness becomes a virtue, we're in deep trouble.

Those of us caught up in frenetic living require strategies to guide us to an alternative. On a hike, or a walk in a park, when you sense yourself hurrying or tangled in thought as you clomp along, walk slowly for a few minutes. Better yet, stop for a minute. Take a few breaths. *Listen.* Do you hear any birds? What is this place saying to you? Is a breeze hitting your face? Can you smell the ground or any of the vegetation around you? What's the taste in your mouth? Take a few slow steps and really feel your shoe contacting the ground, your weight shifting, your back foot rising and swinging forward into the next step. If going steeply uphill, take a rest step by locking your back leg with most of your weight on it, pause, then step forward onto the front foot. This can be a form of walking meditation, what Japanese Zen practitioners call *kinhin.*

Checking in with each of your senses can enhance your awareness of your body and everything that's happening around you there in the forest or in your garden. It may even help you begin to slow down and generate what Gerald May has called "the power of the slowing," a slowing of both the body and the mind.

As I hike along the Dry River, I direct my attention away from education debates and toward the rocks on the trail and sensations in my legs. My quads are swelling, my feet are starting to get hot, and I give myself to the act of walking. In this way, hiking provides an opportunity to practice what Dōgen, the founder of Sōtō Zen in

Japan, calls *gūjin* ("thoroughly and exhaustively"): the act of pouring yourself completely into what you're doing, whether breathing in meditation or sweeping, raking, wiping verandas with wet rags, or other forms of *samu*, labor around the monastery. On the trail, give yourself to the physicality of hiking: to breathing, to taking steps with full attention, to maintaining a slow and steady pace. As I do this along a gently rising section of the trail, my act of walking becomes my destination, not Mount Pierce, not the munchies waiting in the car, not a cold beer in Lincoln.

A few minutes later the trail leaves the river to wind around a cliff that rises thirty feet above the river. As I hike up the steep incline, my lungs remind me that breathing is our most basic life activity. Each day we inhale and exhale over 15,000 times. "Respiration" derives from *spiritus*, Latin for "breath," similar to the Greek word *pneuma*: "breath," "spirit," and in some cases, "soul." While we live, we respire. When we die, we expire—we stop breathing, and the spiritus leaves the body. If we are spiritual, we may be lucky enough to gain inspiration, a breath of creative air that is breathed into us by the Great Spirit or some other form of the divine. Hindus situate *praṇā*, the breath, at the center of yoga, which shares an Indo-European root with "yoke," as in yoking a horse or yoking one's untamed breath, body, and mind while on a mat in an ashram or yoga studio.

Most Buddhist meditation teachers tell us to focus on the breath. Inhaling and exhaling, we feel how our body is always breathing, a primal spontaneous activity that keeps us alive as we go about our business. But with our monkey minds cackling and swinging from thought to thought, we may find that focusing on the breath isn't easy. One suggestion is to count our exhalations, from one to ten, and then from one again. This can facilitate absorption in the act of breathing, what Zen calls *sūsokkan*, literally, "the contemplation that consists of counting one's breath."

Whether on a trail or a city street, walk at a pace where you can keep your breath settled. Move slowly enough that you don't get out of breath and fall into rapid, shallow breathing in your chest. In other words, keep your pace one notch lower than your enthusiasm desires. Gradually you may find yourself flowing across the landscape, like the breeze I saw back in 1976 that painted calligraphic swirls in an iridescent rice field outside that apartment in Izumisano.

After clearing the ravine, the trail descends back to the river. I roll down the slope. My knees are relieved each time I level off on a terrace. As I undulate down, I can hear the river as it, too, glides over the landscape. My imagination kicks in, and I see the ground rising up to meet my boots. It's as if the White Mountains are undulating along with me and the river as we all flow in different directions. Dōgen tells us in his *Sansuikyō* (Mountains and Waters Sutra) that "blue mountains are constantly walking." Here in this valley today, everything is in motion.

As I accelerate down the last stretch to the riverbank—maybe too quickly for my own good—my sense of self shifts from hiker to animal. To walk in the woods is to be reminded that we are embodied animals, grunting, eating berries, sweating, peeing, diving naked into frigid pools, taking part in the communal dance of deer, raccoons, and bears. We also bang into things. Rocks scrape our shins. Branches poke us. Poison ivy sends our skin into blistered mayhem. Mosquitoes bite us. As we plug in to nature, nature plugs in to us.

Most of the time other animals are peripheral to our lives. They are "out there" in nature, except when they intrude into our habitat: mice in the house, raccoons toppling trashcans, bears destroying bird feeders. When hiking, we're in their habitat, and we occupy an unfamiliar and unsettling niche in the food chain. Perhaps this is why our instincts become clearer and more insistent when we're in the woods. Our heads turn abruptly when we hear rustling beyond the light of the fire or when a sound near our sleeping bag jolts us awake. I recall an experience back in 1974 on another backpacking trip, about which I wrote in my journal,

> Above the Yosemite Valley, beside Snow Creek trail. Food hung, I'm sleeping on the ground. Gray light an hour before sunrise. An oinking sound. Pig dream. The oinking prods me awake. Not a pig. A black bear, sniffing and snorting at the foot of my sleeping bag. No food there. Just me, smelly from three hours on sun-baked switchbacks up and out of the valley the day before. Startled, I let out a yell. The bear jumps back, and decides to waddle away through some trees. I stay on my back, looking up at branches and sky. Then, from down the trail, voices: "Get out of here. Damn. The bear's got my pack. Drop it. Get. Get! Get out of here!"

As I was reminded that morning more than forty years ago, vulnerable as I slept under the stars, I am a body, some meat available for other creatures. Today, as a body I am hiking up toward Oakes Gulf. As the Chinese have mapped, the *qi* energy coursing through my body mirrors the larger flow of energy through this landscape. I am a microcosm of the macro-universe. Blake taught us to "see a world in a grain of sand" and the Chinese taught us to see it in our bodies, which are as amazing as the changing of the seasons, planetary motion, and the Crab Nebula.

An hour into the hike I come to a sturdy suspension bridge that was rebuilt several years ago. Sixty feet long and six feet wide, it starts bouncing as I near the center. Through cracks between the planks I can see the not-so-dry Dry River eight feet below, surging over a jumble of boulders. I wonder what would happen if I were to fall in. Could I release my hip belt quickly enough? Would my head get smashed against a rock? Where would my body end up?

Sweat soaks the bandana around my head, making me look and feel like an overworked sushi chef. On the far side of the bridge I take off my pack and swig on my water bottle, a more attractive option than drinking out of a "bladder." As I chug, I'm reminded that I am 70 percent water. A Zen novice is called an *unsui*, "clouds and water," or perhaps better translated "cloud-water," drifting effortlessly across an empty sky. Standing by the bridge, I remember once feeling like a rain cloud, as I hiked up to Spray Park on the west side of Mount Rainier. It was August, and unusually hot for the Northwest, back before I started attributing such weather to climate disruption. As I trudged up the west side of the volcano, sweat gushed from my pores. (At least it seemed like it was gushing.) An hour later I stripped off my clothes and swam in Mowich Lake. I then lay on a rock, with the sun warming my face and a twig poking my back. Water on my chest evaporated quickly in the dry heat.

One Buddhist cosmology sees nature as composed of four basic elements: water, earth, fire, and wind/air. Water is the element of fluidity and cohesion. Moisture rides warm updrafts, forming thunderheads over Mount Jefferson, and by this evening lightning may escort the water back down. A stream shoots off the cliff at Bridalveil Falls, fans out, and reunites down below the boulders. Lenticular slabs hover above Glacier Peak. The Amazon snakes out of the Andes. I guzzle from a Nalgene bottle and the water slides down my parched throat. Sweat beads up on my forehead. I piss behind a tree. From cloud to rain to pond to river to water bottle to stomach to bladder (the one *inside* my body) to foamy yellow puddle disappearing in the pine needles a few feet from where one of the bridge cables is anchored in the ground.

Earth is solidity—a chunk of gneiss in the river, the pack riding on my shoulders and hips, the oatmeal eaten at breakfast, the bagel to be eaten for midday carbs, the ramen at the end of the day. Soil to grain to bagel to poop to soil. Earth is my body, heavy when I slide into a bug bivy under the moon. Both hikers and Zen practitioners value being "down to earth" and "grounded" rather than "tipsy" or "floating" with one's "head in the clouds." As humans we are like humus, the organic part of soil, and we may be descendants of Adam, from the Hebrew word *ādhām*, red earth.

Fire is the element of heat. Fusion in the sun generates hot light, which then travels about eight minutes to get here and radiate off ledges. On frosty nights heat pulsates out of coals and collects in my down bag. Today, early in this hike, warm air lingers between my skin and polypro shirt.

Air is mobility. It swirls around Lhotse and delivers weather fronts to the unsuspecting climber. A blessed breeze cooled me a few summers ago when I grunted up the switchbacks leading to Garnet Canyon below the Middle Teton. Cursed breezes deliver hypothermia to those stuck in wet layers as the temperature plunges during a summer whiteout in Huntington Ravine. Updrafts suspend hawks above the ridge to my left and lift moisture into thunderheads. The air in today's drainage, as I breathe it in, and out, animates me, an animal, with an *anima*, a soul—or without one, depending on how Buddhist I'm feeling.

In my Daoist moments, as I breathe, I think about the two modes of qi, *yin* and *yang*. When I hike, I feel energy moving through me and my surroundings in these two modes. Tucked deep in the valley, getting my first glimpses of the Oakes Gulf headwall, I feel the dampness around me—a highly yin location. Cool air hovers above the brook, and the water flows over carpets of thick moss. The *Daodejing* views the Dao as a creative force tucked into hidden recesses like this stretch of the trail: "The spirit of the valley never dies. This is called the mysterious female."[45] Though it is midday, the trail is in the shade here, a far cry from where I was on a hike several weeks ago.

On that hike I climbed Mount Lafayette from the south. I walked along the spine of the dragon, following its undulations from Mount Flume, along Mount Liberty, Little Haystack, and Mount Lincoln to the summit of Lafayette, where its rocky head gazes north to Canada. You may see its breath, drifting out over the Pemigewasset Wilderness, nudged by the prevailing west wind that makes the White Mountains so brutal in winter. Its southwest flank gets warmed by the afternoon sun, and the northeast shoulder drops down to the shady banks of Lincoln Brook as it winds around Owl's Head in the center of the Pemi. Up on the summit of Lafayette that day, the rocks were dry and surprisingly warm as they soaked up the June sunshine—a fully yang spot. The view west expanded across the Connecticut River Valley to the Green Mountains, and to the east the Presidentials jutted up on the far side of Crawford Notch. The Pemi was deep in shadow, its coolness calling to me as I wiped away the sweat that was stinging my eyes. I pulled my water bottle from a pouch on the side of my pack. As I took a swig, I could see why the Chinese have claimed that mountain topography reveals the flow of qi through the landscape.

Today, as I relish this shaded section of the Dry River Trail, I find myself thinking about how yin and yang also connote stillness and movement. I sometimes find myself repeating a mantra of sorts: "Sit like a mountain and move like a puma." In meditation, I sit in my own pyramidal form, like the upper reaches of Everest: butt and crossed legs planted firmly on a cushion or the ground, my torso and head tapering upward—solid, weathered, resisting the wind and rain. My inner animist imagines a totem animal: the puma, whose other names include cougar, mountain lion, and catamount. On and off the trail I try to move like one—fluidly, quietly, with suppleness, like flowing water. With balance and strength, pumas glide across boulder fields, exemplifying the Zen notion of *fūryū*, usually translated as elegance but literally meaning "wind flow" or, better yet, "flowing like the wind." The stalking done by mountain lions, as Gerald May points out, "requires a keen, open, unfocused awareness of landscape, scents, wind shifts, and a host of other perceptions all at once; it simply *must* be contemplative."[46] Though I have a sense of this awareness, I have not had a puma vision, or any vision like those that young Lakotas have after fasting for several days in the Black Hills. Nevertheless, cougars have inhabited my dreams for decades, and in some of those dreams I have inhabited cougar bodies.

I've always been drawn to cats. In kindergarten, I got a cat named Rusty. Living up to the aphorism, this cat had nine lives, or at least two, as I discovered one day in first grade.

When I found her in the gutter, I didn't notice right away that her head was banged in. All I knew was that Rusty was limp and peppered with dirt. Daylight was slipping away, taking Rusty's life with it.

I ran up the lawn to the front door and shouldered it open. "Mom, Dad. Come quick." My father jumped up from his recliner in the den and flung the newspaper down on the cushion. "What happened?"

"Rusty's lyin' in the road and not movin'."

My dad hustled down behind me to the street, his deerskin slippers squishing as they absorbed the sogginess of the late-March lawn.

I reached Rusty first, and crouched behind her as my father stepped into the street. Perhaps seeing the dent in her skull, he inadvertently blurted out, "Oh God," then "Let me get the car."

As he hurried back into the house to get his keys, I huddled over Rusty, afraid to touch her yet wanting to shake her awake, back into my little world in northwestern Connecticut. I kept my butt to the road, a fragile barrier protecting her from the cars zooming down Norfolk Road from North Street.

A peaceful afternoon of damming rivers that flowed from a mound of dirty snow had been ripped down the middle. Shaking there on the side of the road, I entered the surreal dreaminess that follows shock.

My fugue was pierced by the engine turning over in the gray Nash Rambler. Pop ran down the driveway with the army surplus blanket he kept with the box of sand in the trunk of the car and cradled Rusty in the green layers of wool. He laid her on the back seat, and for the first time I could see the streaks of blood along her cheek.

On the way to the clinic Pop fidgeted as he drove, pushing up the visor to flatten it against the ceiling, offering me a breath mint, and fingering coins he kept in a compartment below the radio. Maybe he was scared, too, or simply trying to distract his six-year-old son from the inevitability waiting down the road.

We pulled into a circular driveway in front of a white building, and Dr. Wallace emerged in a lab coat, alerted by a call from my mother. He opened the back door of the car and reached down, his forearms moving like the prongs of a forklift. As he picked Rusty up, he said, a bit too casually for my taste, "Hi Bud. Marilla just called. Let's take Rusty inside. Okay Chris?"

As we entered the clinic, I was hit by the chemical smell and the yelping of caged dogs. Rusty's legs hung rubbery over Dr. Wallace's arms, and he backed through a swinging door to the examination room. As he disappeared into the bright chamber, he asked us to wait in the reception area.

In a few minutes he emerged, and with forced enthusiasm said, "Well, I've started taking care of her, Chris, and I'm going to need to keep her overnight. You and your dad should go home now, and I'll call in the morning. There're some lollipops in the basket over there. Help yourself."

By this point my brain had started to secrete the chemicals it had at its disposal to subdue fear, and I walked numbly over to his receptionist's desk. Seeing that my focus had shifted to the flat suckers in their plastic wrapping, Dr. Wallace mumbled something to my father. Years later I would learn what he said: "Bud, you see what sort of shape she's in. There's little I can do, but I'll clean her up and try to make her comfortable."

That night my sleep was chopped up by dreams of tornadoes and mutant animals coming out of the woods. When the phone rang at 7:30 the next morning, I was tangled in the covers, neither awake nor asleep.

Mom picked up the phone on the wall next to the refrigerator, and Dr. Wallace was there on the other end of the line. He said something like, "Hello, Marilla. You can come get Rusty. When I came into the clinic this morning, she was up in her cage screaming for food. Her head popped out in the night. I don't know what to make of it, but she seems fine."

Perhaps at a year old her skull was still soft and her brain yielding, at least in the moment a front tire struck her. Whatever the reason, Rusty was in fact fine, and she returned that day to her world—my world—on Norfolk Road, to napping in the garage, prowling through the woods, and hunting the birds at my mother's feeder outside the kitchen window.

Rusty lived another eighteen years, until I was three years out of college. We never could housebreak her, and she never approached the road again.

As I get older, I'm continually reminded that my body is not that of a lithe housecat or cougar. And yet, as I start to ascend the old rail bed up the east bank of the Dry River, I feel grateful for the body I have, and for how, even with all the aches, it continues to serve me on my hikes.

Several years ago when I moved from the Northwest to Boston, away from "big nature" out west to the confines of the urbanized East Coast, I felt dis-located, a bit homeless. To stay grounded, I kept reminding myself, again in mantra fashion, that my ultimate home is my body. It's a mobile home, a moving monastery. In traditional

Zen monasteries the buildings are laid out in correspondences with the body parts of the Buddha. The abbot's chamber is seen as the head, the Buddha hall the heart, the monks' hall the left arm, the kitchen the right arm, the latrine the left leg, the bathhouse the right leg, and the mountain gate the groin.[47] At some point I could lose my material possessions, but I can invest in my body, and maybe even treat it as sacred space. I know how to exercise, and I have time to do it. I have access to healthy food. I'm lucky enough to have insurance for medical care.

Hiking is all about the body and the physicality of things encountered along the trail. On the far side of a feeder stream about two and half miles up the valley, a jagged erratic, the size of the eighteen-foot rental truck I once helped a friend load, lords over the trail. Exposed to wind and snow for 12,000 years, the boulder is clothed in lichen and glittered with yellow hemlock needles. Though not as stunning as the two-story boulder that Mishy and I walked past in Kings Canyon several years ago, it exudes power. In my chest I feel the bulk of this rock. It towers over me, intimidating, and at the same time making me aware of my own physicality, my own strength as I walk around it and find myself towering over ferns on its shady side. If I were a Japanese person a thousand years ago, the impression the rock gives me—of something powerful, out of the ordinary, and awe inspiring—would have me imagine the presence of a kami.

Maybe the ants crossing the trail here view humans as awe inspiring, too. They may even see us as kami. Or maybe as monsters, pure and simple. But like Shintō gods, our power has limits. No omnipotence, but enough oomph to move up the trail, to present ourselves to this boulder, to tower over the ants.

A few minutes farther up the path, I notice that my right trapezius is getting sore under the straps. As with other pilgrims, this physical pain has value. It reminds me that right now I am on the trail, in my body, tucked into a valley on the south side of the Presidentials. And it reminds me of other times on the trail, in pain, in joy.

FOUR

Letting Go

手を放す

TE O HANASU —
"RELEASE ONE'S GRIP"

> Unlike a typical adventurer, the pilgrim seeks not to conquer the worlds he visits but to surrender to them; and unlike a missionary, he seeks not to preach but, in the silence of his supplication, to listen.
>
> —PICO IYER[48]

> Since all our troubles are caused by our discriminating minds, we should open the hand of thought. This is *shinjin datsuraku*—body and mind falling off. That is when all our troubles disappear.
>
> —KŌSHŌ UCHIYAMA[49]

S OME DAYS I'M CONTENT to head out to the garden, stroll along a river, or walk in a local forest. Other times, like today, I feel drawn to hike up into a more remote area. But why do I go into the backcountry? A lot of us seek natural places to prove something, to show how brave and tough we are. "We hiked twenty-five miles that day with an elevation gain of 6,000 feet." "A few kilometers from Chamonix I did a 5.12 with some dicey overhangs." "We had to downclimb in whiteout conditions." "She thru-hiked the Appalachian Trail in record time." "I bagged three peaks this afternoon."

Nowadays nature serves many people as a place to build up the ego, not as a place to let go of it. Granted, many of those who find new routes up vertical faces outside Moab, do first runs on Class V rapids in China, or bag all fourteen of the 8,000-meter peaks, do so with humility, and surely they appreciate the natural wonders around them. But many of those who head out—or talk about heading out—seem focused on other things.

Well aware of this, gear companies clean up on those seeking to bolster their egos or get an adrenaline rush. Glossy catalogues display climbers on knife-edge ridges in Torres del Paine. Spreads in *Outside* magazine advertise the newest North Face jacket and the innovative line of ultralight gear that can get us quickly to the top of the Eiger.

And then there's the commercialization and commodification of outdoor activities. When I was a kid, we made up our own games, using trees, sticks, the random can to be kicked, and mounds of snow (being skinny and on the short side, I never excelled at King of the Mountain). Now much of our experience in nature is mediated by monetary transactions.

Though haunted by advertising, commercialization, and the hype of the X Games, venturing into the woods does provide a chance to let go. In the backcountry we can free ourselves from our gadgets and the addictive apps we recently downloaded to them. Not that this is easy. There's a summer camp in northern California for adults who can't do this on their own, and a *Frontline* episode about treating computer addicts in China.

Heading out on the trail also provides an opportunity to unlearn bad habits. In Gary Snyder's idiom, we can de-educate ourselves. Like other pilgrims, we remove ourselves from unhealthy behaviors, constrictive routines, and complicated relationships. I sometimes do a visualization exercise in which I imagine putting these parts of life down on the ground at the trailhead. Or leaving them in a pile next to my car, with an eye toward picking up whatever seems worthwhile—and only that—at the end of the hike.

At the very least, once we pass through the threshold into the woods and start hiking, we can extricate ourselves from the scattered multitasking that fills too many of our days. Ideally, we're just walking. Thoreau once wrote, "work earnestly, though it be at cleaning a table."[50] Perhaps familiar with this virtue in his friend, Emerson once wrote that Thoreau "knew but one secret which was to do but one thing at a time."[51]

This echoes something I mentioned earlier: Dōgen's notion of gūjin, the pouring of oneself into the action at hand. As we all know, we are not born with a switch that turns off monkey mind and puts us in a state of calm. But what we can do is, like Thoreau, give ourselves fully to what we're doing. This is why so many of us find relief in working out, playing the piano, and pursuing hobbies to which we can devote our full attention. They are our sanctuary, an effective way of granting ourselves at least a temporary break from worries. And when we immerse ourselves in a favorite activity, with passion, we burn cleanly.

In this way we leave no trace, though not simply in the backpacking sense of choosing campsites carefully, pooping appropriately, and carrying out all of our trash (including, in the case of ultra-purists, the poop). I'm thinking of what Zen means by leaving no trace (mu-seki), which has less to do with one's physical surroundings than with pouring oneself into an action and then moving on to the next action, without residual attachment to outcome or accolades. Zen master Shunryu Suzuki once said, "When you do something, you should burn yourself completely, like a good bonfire, leaving no trace of yourself."[52] Do things one at a time, with focus, and move gracefully through your day without breaking things. Show up each moment with no investment in making your mark or trying to prove something, and with as much savvy and compassion as you can muster, just do what needs to be done. Then let go.

As I move along the Dry River Trail, in a steady rhythm, I feel myself starting to settle. My breath is steady, and my attention is on the rocks and roots in the trail. I feel the muggy air and the stiffness in my fingers caused by reduced circulation. Though I'm not in any special state of consciousness, I'm definitely here in my body.

When, like today, we step back from our habitual, obsessive, and perhaps frenetic patterns and give ourselves to the physical act of hiking, to the smell of pine needles, to the sun on our forehead, and to the taste of water, our thoughts and worries quiet down and our mind opens up. Sights and sounds start to fill us. We can better attend to whatever presents itself to us. And not just things outside us. Internally, thoughts or worries may still arise, but we don't hang on to them. We let them pass. Or as Zen master Kōshō Uchiyama puts it, we "open the hand of thought."

Like hiking, pilgrimages nudge us to let go. Leaving the security of home, workplace, and daily routine and pursuing what the theologian Paul Tillich refers to as "ultimate concern," pilgrims accept risk, psychological and physical. We may be attacked by doubts and by those who desire our money, possessions, or body. We may get bogged down in John Bunyan's "slough of despond." We may get so dislocated that we'll end up deranged, from French, *déranger*, from *de-reng*, "deplaced or displaced"—cut off from one's home range.

The letting go of security may even be absolute: leaving not just our comfort zone but life itself. When circumambulating the island of Shikoku with stops at eighty-eight temples associated with miracles by the renowned saint Kūkai,[53] pilgrims wear a white garment analogous to the shroud placed over a corpse. They also don a bamboo hat, symbolizing their coffin, and written inside the hat is a poem about impermanence that usually appears on coffins. As they walk mile after mile in straw sandals, they carry only a staff, representing their gravestone. "Thus symbolically dressed for death, wearing their shroud and carrying their gravestone and coffin, pilgrims are symbolically in the realm of death as they travel."[54] In a similar vein, a marathon monk on Mount Hiei carries a knife and a "cord of death" on his circumambulations, in case he needs to take his own life for failing to complete the ascetic practice, and into his rectangular straw hat he tucks a coin to cover the cost of being ferried across the Sanzu River in the underworld.[55] Thoreau, too, recognized pilgrims' unflinching spirit: "We should go forth on the shortest walk, perchance, in the spirit of undying adventure, never to return—prepared to send back our embalmed hearts only as relics to our desolate kingdoms."[56]

The imagery of death also symbolizes how pilgrimage strips us of our identities "back in the world." We sever contact with our work, wear the same attire as other pilgrims, move equally as children of God or recipients of a saint's blessing, and in this liminal state we "die" as our ordinary self with all of its roles, status, and wealth (or lack thereof), as well as its worries, judgments, greed, and anger. In lifting us up and out of our concerns, pilgrimage—and hiking—may also elevate us into communion with something higher. We may even get born again.

When the pilgrim separates from home, she is usually making some sort of sacrifice, from *sacr-*, "sacred," and *facere*, "to make." Though "sacrifice" implies relinquishing things that give us comfort and accepting pain, with this etymology it connotes the act of sanctifying something—maybe even oneself. This sanctification may go hand in hand with purification. Typical pilgrimage strips away possessions to a prescribed level of simplicity and restrains our eating, drinking, and sexual activity, putting us into a state of purity more sustained than the temporary ritual purity achieved by leaving jewelry and gadgets at home when we go to our place of worship or washing our hands, feet, and mouth before prayer. Male pilgrims to Mecca put themselves in a state of *ihram*—purity and consecration—by changing into two white pieces of cloth and refraining from sex, smoking, anger, oaths, and conflict during the hajj.

On a hike, through the sacrificial, sanctifying act of stripping possessions down to a minimum, letting go of the creature comforts at home, and following a simple plan, we can extricate ourselves from common forms of mental impurity: getting caught up in possessions, obsessing about electronic communications, and scheduling every moment in our day. Thanks to the repetitive rhythm of walking along with a pack, we can let go of that obsessiveness when we're on the trail.

FIVE

Ritualizing a Walk

....

Ritual allows us to transcend our individual selves to gain a
sense of participation with the greater environment of the
forces controlling our singular and communal destinies.

—JOHN NELSON[57]

FOR SEVERAL MILES above the suspension bridge the trail
continues up the valley on an abandoned railroad bed. In the
nineteenth century the Dry River drainage was logged clear up to
Oakes Gulf, and as I hike past hemlocks, haircap moss, and cinna-
mon ferns, I realize that my energy is low and my mind groggy as
it roams over concerns about ticks, mosquitoes carrying Eastern
equine encephalitis, my mother's atrial fibrillation, how I'm going
to get my students engaged next semester, and stiffness in my right
knee (iliotibial band tight again?). This may not be a day for a peak
experience—in either sense of the expression.

Sometimes on the trail it's hard for me to concentrate on the act of
walking, tune in to my senses, and savor the natural beauty around
me. I can be lost in my head, thinking about tension with a colleague
or the pain in my right big toe. I start obsessing about my love han-
dles bulging above the hip belt, feeling angry with myself for not
shaking the ten extra pounds I've been vowing to get rid of for the
past twenty years. Then I shift into jock mode, seeing the hike as
a good workout, thinking about how many miles I've hiked, how
many more to go, how many minutes per mile, how many feet of
elevation gain, how the hike stacks up relative to a half-marathon.

57

Or my ego kicks in, attached to appearing fit and savvy when I cross paths with other hikers.

On this muggy and buggy morning I recognize that pilgrimages do not always trigger dramatic experiences of nature or beatific visions of the divine. At the very least, though, I want to shake the worrying that accompanied me on the way up from Boston on Route 93.

At times like this, silence can help. When hiking with others, I find that spreading out along the trail provides the physical and auditory space necessary for quieting down. If I need a break, I try to find a place that speaks to me, a spot that is beautiful or feels powerful. Then, while hydrating or munching some trail mix, I try to sit quietly, with the woods as my meditation hall, and the trees, rocks, birds, bugs, and critters as my sangha, my monastic community of fellow beings. By sitting quietly I can be more open to and aware of their presence.

I may try doing seated meditation beside the trail. Here's how I recently described it to a curious student.

Take off your pack. Find a flat rock about eight inches off the ground. Sit on the front edge, cross your legs comfortably, sit up straight. Touch the ground with your hand to fully contact that place, like the Buddha did when he touched the ground in the "earth-touching gesture" and proclaimed to Māra, "The earth is my witness." Feel that spot as your seat, your version of the place where the Buddha sat, his seat of diamond-sharp wisdom.

Put your right hand down on your lap, palm up. Then place your left hand, palm up, on top of the right, with thumb tips touching. In this position your hands will form a round cradle and be encompassed by your arms as a bigger circle, just like how you are contained in and part of the big circle of the universe.

Let your gaze drop down to a spot on the ground about eighteen inches in front of you. Feel yourself sitting there. A pyramid of flesh and bone, polypro and fleece. Aldo Leopold spoke of "thinking like a mountain," but on a hike try sitting like a mountain. Settle there. Sit with a broad, firm base. Imagine your butt sinking deep into the earth. Feel your chest as a cliff, your shoulders as spurs slanting off the summit cone. Feel the weathered ridge of your nose and the summit on the top of your head. Feel the sun and breeze hitting your slopes. Feel the heat rising off your head. Feel your solidity as you sit there. Feel the aches and sweat.

Breathe in the woods around you. And if you can do it without effort, breathe abdominally, from what Japanese monks and martial artists call the hara, *your center of gravity in the belly, about an inch below your navel. To inhale, gently push out your belly like a rotund Buddha sculpture in a garden, and bring it back in slowly to send the breath out. Feel your breath come in, bringing fresh air, full of oxygen that is being offered by the larches, cedars, and mountain laurel around you. Feel the air slowly leave through your nostrils. Extend your outbreath slightly until your lungs are empty. Offer up the carbon dioxide to the plants around you.*

Then just continue to breathe. Pour yourself into each outbreath. Let sounds enter you and pass through. Be fully there as a mountain.

After five, ten, or thirty minutes, place your palms together in front of your chest and bow. When you start to move again, do one thing at a time. Slowly. Extend your legs. Stand up. Remain still for a minute. Lift your pack and put in on. Latch the hip belt and sternum strap.

When you start walking again, slow your pace 20 percent. Keep it slow, with your breath at ease. And as you continue along the trail and through the day, keep doing just one thing at a time. Give yourself to each step. When wiping your forehead, just wipe your forehead. Just munch the trail mix. Just swig. "Don't wobble."

Needing a few moments to center myself today, I feel drawn to a spot where the Dry River narrows through a gauntlet of boulders and hemlocks. I find a flat ledge. I cross my legs, put my hands in the oval mudra, and take my first deep breath. The cascade tumbles and splashes past me. I recall a verse by the Japanese poet-monk Ryōkan:

> Like the little stream
> Making its way
> Through the mossy crevices,
> I, too, quietly,
> Turn clear and transparent.[58]

Clear and transparent. Still. Formless in my form. Small, and at the same time expanding in all directions. I try to sit like I suggested to my student, like a mountain, grounded in this place.

Another verse, this one from the *Theragatha*, a collection of "verses by elder monks," comes to mind as well:

> As a mountain of rock is unmoving, firmly established,
> so a monk, with the ending of delusion,
> like a mountain, doesn't quake.[59]

When it proves hard to quiet the mind and be fully present on the trail, I try ritualizing the hike in other ways. In addition to bowing at the trailhead, along the way I sometimes pause at the altars:

white pine seedling growing up from a dirt-filled crack on a granite boulder; meltoff gurgling down a foot-wide chasm to the trail; a red maple leaf resting on a carpet of moss, just so, far beyond the skills of the most renowned ikebana master in Kyoto.

Scattered on the flanks of Mount Hiei, the de facto altars where the marathon monks pray are spots where a person long ago sensed something out of the ordinary, something awe inspiring and perhaps even a bit intimidating, what German thinker Rudolf Otto described as a mysterious power (*mysterium*) that is both scary (*tremendum*) and fascinating (*fascinans*). The Israelites experienced this as they stood trembling in fear and awe at the base of Mount Sinai, encountering the thunderous manifestation of the divine. When early Japanese had such an experience, they concluded that the spot was the abode of a kami.

But we don't need to be a marathon monk or a Shintō believer looking up at the summit of Mount Fuji to feel mystery and awe. If we can pay attention, power spots are all around us. Not only Mount Rainier, the north face of the Eiger, or Niagara Falls, but a maple tree towering over Boston Common.

Whatever is it, when something catches your attention on the trail—with distinctive beauty, power, or mystery—try bowing to it, even if you feel self-conscious doing so. Show respect to the geological and biological forces presenting themselves. Today I pause to spend a moment with a delicate mountain laurel flower that has caught my eye on the side of the trail; I exhale and let that one thing fill me, then bow slightly as I continue up the trail.

I imagine the whole system of which the flower is a part, the supernova that created the molecules of the mountain laurel flower, the creation of soil from the erosion of rocks, the seed that fell in that place, the light from the sun that generated the leaves. That single white flower is a gate to the whole. Before I turn away, I bow to it once more in reverence and say a word of gratitude.

I didn't always attend to little things in this way. I used to seek the grand and dramatic in my hikes—the vertical walls of Yosemite, the sprawling glaciers on the south side of Mount Baker, winds roaring through the Columbia River gorge, the terrifying blocks of ice tumbling down the Khumbu Icefall. Living now in New England, my focus has perforce shifted to micro-beauty (not that the Presidentials are a minor geological hiccup).

A few hundred yards beyond the mountain laurel, just after the Mount Clinton Trail branches to the left across the river and up to the Mizpah Hut, I pause to take in my surroundings. Here, about three miles up the trail, a lady's slipper droops in my direction, as if to give me an embrace, and an admiral butterfly zigzags its way over the river. With the help of endorphins and several hours of staying with my breath, I can better appreciate how each of these things manifests itself. As I start walking again, a clump of ghost pipe bows to me. A minute or so later, I thank a patch of hobblebush for holding its leaf hands up on either side of a sunny stretch of trail, directing me through its celebratory canyon. A half mile later I nod to a bunchberry colony for blessing my foray into their soggy neighborhood. Today, these are my *kalyāṇamitra*, my companions on the path. With the words, "May you flourish," I extend *mettā*, loving-kindness, to them.

To augment these traditional Buddhist practices, when on the trail I sometimes make up hiker chants: "one step at a time"; "I am a critter, too." The mantra that comes to mind on this hike is "This valley is my home, too." Chanting this prompts me to think about my neighbors here. I scan the plants around me and try to imagine how they support my existence. I do a mental inventory of the animals that might live in this drainage. I think about how I affect them, in the ongoing dance of energy, in what Snyder calls a grand sacramental exchange, a potlatch of all the species. This helps me follow the insight meditation teacher Mark Coleman's advice to "practice participating in nature instead of simply observing it."[60]

Needless to say, we can ritualize our hikes in whatever way serves our spiritual path. There is a group of people who have been doing precisely that for a thousand years in Japan: the *yamabushi* (山伏), literally, "those who lie down in the mountains." Drawing from Buddhist practices and Shintō beliefs that mountains are the realm of the dead and other spirits, these masters of ritualized hiking "enter the peaks" to practice "the path of austerities," *shugendō*. They engage in a prescribed set of actions that are believed to transform them into a buddha, right there in their current bodies. Similar to the marathon monks, these ascetics transform speech through mantras, the body through hand positions or mudras, and the mind through mandalas. The mandalas portray the legion of buddhas surrounding the cosmic sun buddha, Vairochana, and provide a map of the cosmos that is simultaneously a map for the practitioner's journey along the Buddhist path. As the scholar Max Moerman puts it, "The mandala spatializes Buddhist thought. It provides the tools for drawing the cosmos into the ceremonial act and for establishing correspondences between the deity and the practitioner, between the macrocosm and the microcosm."[61]

In Shingon, the Japanese denomination closest to Tibetan Buddhism, there are two main mandalas, portraying the Diamond Realm and the Womb Realm. Working with the former, the practitioner attains Vairochana's diamond-sharp wisdom. Through the latter mandala, as implied by the womb imagery, the person is born anew and emerges out in the world with compassionate concern for others. This parallels the iconography of one of the patron buddhas of the yamabushi, Fudō Myō'ō, whose rope and sword, and the flames at his back, represent the compassionate lassoing, excision, and burning away of the attachments of the old self, which, through rigorous practices in the mountains, must die a spiritual death. The two mandalas can also represent what one Zen master refers to as contraction and expansion, not only as the two basic movements of the cosmos but also as the inbreath and outbreath.

In the case of the yamabushi, the mandala is mapped not only on the practitioner but on the natural setting around him. Long ago the Diamond Realm and Womb Realm mandalas were superimposed on the landscape of Ōmine, the mountainous spine of the Kii Peninsula southeast of Kyoto. Peaks there were linked to buddhas in the mandalas and to the mantras and rituals associated with each of those awakened beings. As Gary Snyder learned while "walking the great ridge Ōmine on the womb-diamond trail" in 1968, at a time when the paths had become choked with weeds and hard to follow, diamond and womb "are descriptive of two complementary but not exactly dichotomous ways of seeing the world, and representative of such pairs as mind/environment, evolutionary drama/ecological stage, mountains/waters, compassion/wisdom, the Buddha as enlightened being/the world as enlightened habitat, etc."[62]

In those mountains, at spots corresponding to where particular buddhas or bodhisattvas are painted on the mandalas, the yamabushi chant prayers and incantations directed at tapping the powers of those awakened beings. As they walk along the Ōmine ridge between those places, they recite such texts as the Heart Sutra or chant "*rokkon shōjō*," "purification of the six roots," the six sense organs, which in Buddhist psychology include the mind. You may even hear them chanting, "*zange, zange*," "repentance, repentance."

The yamabushi also chant under waterfalls, sit in meditation, fast, recite sutras to eliminate karmic transgressions, and say prayers to heal the sick. They engage in a ritual called "the practice of throwing away the body," in which they hang upside down over cliffs confessing transgressions and answering questions about their rectitude while other practitioners hold their legs. Luckily for those who do not relish the possibility of weaker comrades releasing them headfirst over the precipice, ropes are tied around their chests as well.

In October of 1965, after experiencing these practices firsthand in Japan, Gary Snyder led Allen Ginsberg and Philip Whalen on a ritualized circuit across the slopes of Mount Tamalpais north of the Golden Gate Bridge in Marin County. Hiking up and along the flanks of the mountain, they chanted the Heart Sutra, the Fourfold Great Vow, verses in praise of Hindu and Buddhist deities, and a Buddhist incantation to avert disasters. They spoke of their practice in Hindu terms as *pradakshina*: circumambulation around sacred sites. Other people picked up what they did that day, and a new tradition was invented.[63]

While on my own hikes, I have recently sensed another new tradition: the construction of cairns, and not just above tree line to guide climbers through fog and snow. I wonder what it is that draws people to make stacks of rocks that serve no practical function, on boulders in the middle of Sabbaday Brook, on the glacial moraine below the Nisqually Glacier, on the rocky beach below Mohegan Bluffs on Block Island.

Today, about four miles up the trail, as I'm forced to bushwhack to splice together the fragments of the trail that remain after eleven inches of Irene rain sent a bulldozer flood down the valley, I find myself wishing someone had erected cairns to guide me. After nearly a mile of stepping over downed trees and scrambling up and down the steep riverbank, I'm relieved to find a surviving stretch of the trail. A short while later, when I no longer need them, I discover a couple of cairns, about a hundred yards below where the Isolation Trail branches up to the right to Davis Path and Bott Spur. They stand in vigil on the bank of the river. Maybe they'll be there the next time I hike up this way, enduring, like the statues of the bodhisattva Jizō that stand at rural crossroads in Japan, protecting travelers. More likely, they will be swept away in next spring's meltoff, or the next time a storm like Hurricane Irene sends a torrent down the Dry River and scours another ten-foot-high gash into the banks.

After twenty more minutes of hiking, I come to a tent site where I have camped with my nephew Josh and my neighbor David. It sits on a slope above the river, just before where the Dry River Cutoff drops down to the river and then rises up to join the Mount Clinton Trail on its way to Mizpah Hut. No one is there at the site. To the west the ridge between Mount Jackson and Mount Pierce rises up, massive and unmoving. Here the valley does seem to merit its description as a "wilderness." Though my car is only six miles away, I feel like I'm in the backcountry. I drop my pack, pull the water bottle from the side pocket, and sit on a log beside the remnants of a fire circle. I feel drawn to spend time in this spot, to savor it rather than continuing on my hike. I look at my watch and see that it's 3:00. I feel the sore spot on my right patella, against which my femur has been rubbing. From some quiet cavern in my psyche rises an urge to spend the night in this place. With that impetus, I unclip the top compartment of the pack and open up the main chamber to dig out the stove and bug bivy.

Like the ritualized actions of tea ceremony, setting up a campsite provides an opportunity to focus on what we are doing in the moment. I start to prepare tonight's home by performing a kind of ritual purification: moving branches and stones away from the tent site. Then I take the bug bivy and the one curving pole out of the stuff sack. I shake out the bivy, lay it out on the ground, and insert the pole to create what will be a mesh canopy above my head and chest. This light and simple structure will be my tent tonight.

On the trail, my tent is my hut, my moving hermitage. Unlike hotels and lean-tos, my shelter, like the feast I carry, is moveable. In accord with impermanence, the hermits in the hills around Kyoto could move their huts, their "temporary dwellings" (*kari no yadori*), whether to dodge visitors from the city, change the view, or avoid getting attached to their beautiful surroundings. Of course, their huts were a different species from the Lakes of the Clouds Hut and the other rock fortresses erected by the Appalachian Mountain Club. In "An Account of My Hut," the recluse monk Kamo no Chō-mei (d. 1216) wrote, "I fastened hinges to the joints of the beams, the easier to move elsewhere should anything displease me."[64] Six centuries later Thoreau said something similar about Indian lodges: "Such a lodge was in the first instance constructed in a day or two at most, and taken down and put up in a few hours."[65]

Though we may think of a hermit as a recluse ensconced for decades in a cabin, Kamo's vision of his hut is steeped in Buddhist notions of impermanence. His "Account" begins, "The flow of the river is ceaseless and the water is never the same. The bubbles that float in the pools, now vanishing, now forming, are not of long duration: so in the world are people and their dwellings."[66] Like the bodies of their inhabitants, homes in the city are subject to decay. Beams sag, foundations crack, wiring needs replacement. In a similar fashion, shoulders sag, bones crack, knees need replacement. My two homes—condo and body—are constantly changing, and in this way set the stage for a core practice on my path: dealing with entropy. Aging loved ones, cars that break down, energy that lags as I enter my sixties, students that doze late in the semester (and early in the semester), roofs that need replacement, feet that need surgery.

Whenever we travel, moving from lodging to lodging, we can attune ourselves to impermanence. Though AMC huts, the chalets above Siusi in the Dolomites, Paradise Lodge on the south side of Rainier, or even the St. Regis Sheraton on 55th Street may endure, the people staying there change daily. In the case of the hermit and the hiker, the hut and the tent change, too, at least in terms of their location.[67] The hermit is fully aware of this transiency and free from the attachments and struggles of life in the city. Kamo writes, "Ever since I fled the world and became a priest, I have known neither hatred nor fear. I leave my span of days for Heaven to determine, neither clinging to life nor begrudging its end. My body is like a drifting cloud—I ask for nothing, I want nothing. My greatest joy is a quiet nap; my only desire for this life is to see the beauties of the seasons."[68]

While at a campsite, it's easy to follow the rhetoric of classical Zen and "chop wood, carry water." We can do chores there as a kind of samu, work practice, fully attending to our labors as we pitch the tent, roll out the pad inside it, put the sheet or sleeping bag on top of the pad, and arrange the food, stove, and canister of propane. We get water from a stream or gather snow to melt; we prepare and eat a meal. Just this.

In Rinzai Zen monasteries, each monk has a set of chopsticks and three bowls (oryoki), stacked and wrapped in a cloth. As the meal begins, the monks unwrap the bowls and set them on the low table at which they sit, chanting the Meal Verse, the Heart Sutra, and statements of gratitude. The servers come along with soup, veggies, and gruel or rice. Each monk hands his bowl to the server and then places his palms together before his sternum. When the bowl has been filled to the desired level, the monk shoots one hand forward, making a swooshing sound against the other palm, and then takes the bowl from the server.

Once all three bowls have been filled and the chants completed, the monks take a few grains of rice or other bits of food and place them on a board that one of the servers brings. This is the offering to gaki, hungry spirits, unfortunate beings who are stuck at a lower level of rebirth because of greed in past lives. They have narrow throats, which thwart their desire and leave them perpetually hungry. The morsels offered to these spirits are usually left outside, where birds and bugs consume them.

The monks then eat in silence, focused on eating, but not slowly. Unlike mindfulness exercises that have us spend minutes gazing at a single raisin before devoting even more minutes to chewing it, the monks devour their food. After they have finished, only two or three minutes after they started, a server returns with a bowl of *takuan* daikon radish pickles—for some reason named after Zen master Takuan (1573-1645)—and each monk takes one and places it in the first bowl, into which a server then pours tea. Using their chopsticks to push the pickle slice around on the inside of the bowl like a sponge, the monks wash that bowl. Then they pour the tea and pickle into the second bowl, and clean it, too. After repeating this one more time with the third bowl, the monks drink the tea—in effect the dishwater—and eat the yellow pickle. Then they wipe the bowls with a cloth, stack them, and wrap them back up in a larger cloth for storage until the next meal.

No waste, no conversation. Mindful eating, ritualized to help the monks give themselves fully to this most basic of human activities.

Today, at this spot above the Dry River, after setting up the bug bivy and taking a nap, I ritualize my meal, too. After I light the stove, I give my full attention to putting the pot on the metal arms of the stove, boiling the water, adding the ramen, putting the lid back on the pot. Not unlike the ritual actions in a tea ceremony. Once the noodles are cooked, I turn the stove off and use my bandana to lift the pot and put in on the ground. I add the contents of the flavor packet and shavings from the chunk of pecorino. I stir everything with my spork, take a bite, and savor the taste of the cheese. Delicious. Nothing to distract me. Though I do sweep a mosquito off my forearm.

To the west, the ridge hides the beginning of the sunset, but the sky above it is saffron, as if an orange wave were hitting the far side of the ridge and splashing up and over it. Tucked in the valley, I feel my separation from what Japanese hermits call the "dusty world"—

life in society—I recline against a log, a contented pilgrim, savoring my carb-filled dinner.

Here and there the last remnants of the cheese are too caked on the pot to remove with my right index finger—which I deploy effectively in lieu of a takuan pickle—so I get up on my stiff legs and walk back to the stream by the trail, fill the pot with water and a handful of sand and gravel, and walk into the woods to scour. An ancient monk attained enlightenment when he heard the sound of a stream. I hear this stream, too, behind the rattle of pebbles as I scrub the pot.

On my way back to the tent site I get swarmed by a legion of mosquitoes, who motivate me to corral my no-impact scruples and grab some fallen branches for a fire. There is something primordial in the gesture of collecting firewood, making a temporary circle of rocks, and starting a fire. For thousands of years (or so it feels to me) humans have been piling kindling—stick shavings, tiny twigs, birch bark, parched duff from the forest floor, lint from the clothes dryer back home—and surrounding it with sticks. I get simple pleasure from keeping the fire going: adding more branches, putting the unburned ends of branches into the center, blowing on coals to revive the flames.

Gazing through the flames into embers on camping trips over fifty years ago in my youth was my first experience of meditation. Some have speculated that meditation began with hunting, when people—usually men, while the women gathered the bulk of the calories that kept the group alive—sat still for hours, paying close attention to what they saw, heard, and smelled around them. Or perhaps meditation started with fishing, which through my youth was my passion—usually down behind Forman School along one branch of the Bantam River, where I spent many a spring and summer day, keeping still, and quiet, on rocks and logs, peering down at my worm and trying not to spook the trout and perch circling it.

On this evening I arrange twigs, then sticks, in a tepee. A faint breeze brushes my face. No sounds except the whoosh of the river. As I light the fire and start adding sticks, I notice that darkness has been thickening around the site.

Whenever I sit by a fire, watching the pulsation in the coals, I feel a connection to those who sat by fires in caves or on the savannah. I feel something ancient. Perhaps it's the elemental reality of fire, its heat, its power of transformation that alchemists and cooks have tapped throughout human history. Maybe the fire is telling me something, in a language too subtle to comprehend. Or maybe the fire gets me in touch with some primal part of myself. Maybe it's what Flynn Johnson has called "our own indigenous soul—the primal, intuitive, embodied part of humanity that lived for many thousands of years in an immediate and intimate connection with the rhythms and beings of the natural world and that still resides within our genetic and spiritual makeup just beneath the thin masks of civilization."[69] Or perhaps while I sit by campfires, I get in touch with something that many of us have lost, what Johnson calls, "glimpses into the soul of the world during childhood—a feeling of a loving presence at the foot of their bed, a magical place in a forest where fairies dwell, a shining light that emanates from the beings around them, the sweet balm of unconditional love."[70]

Or maybe it's simply because I'm out in the woods at night. Rather than the light and warmth of the fire, perhaps it's the darkness and cold of the surrounding woods that gives me those glimpses. The mountain guide and nature philosopher Jack Turner writes, "The easiest way to experience a bit of what the wild was like is to go into a great forest at night alone. Sit quietly for a while. Something very old will return."[71]

In the backcountry I've had at least one other primal feeling: that there might actually be spirits, or kami perhaps, watching me as I walk, or drifting alongside me, just off the trail. Tonight I imagine them beyond the sphere of light projected out by the fire. Maybe it isn't spirits or ghosts but traces of things that happened or people who lived in the distant past. I remember once standing in the doorway to what had been my childhood bedroom many years before, and as I looked at the walls and wooden floors, I felt that at some level, in some parallel dimension, right there in the room, my childhood was happening. I imagined that those with the right eyes could see a ten-year-old setting up battles with plastic army men on the floor. Perhaps it was a lingering echo or some other sort of ripple down to the present.

I often feel nostalgia for my past. It usually takes the form of a longing for the exuberance I felt as a child: the joy of inventing games in the back yard, playing capture the flag with the Boy Scouts, riding waves on inflatable canvas rafts in the surf off Bay Head. At other times it's a longing to recover the primal connection to nature I felt on countless afternoons in the woods. But either way, it's for something lost. Not a golden age, but a past in which I felt more embedded in nature, part of something much larger than myself. Who knows—is this a taste of Jung's collective unconscious? Some thread stretching back along my DNA, a karmic chain to an animal awareness—or nature itself—coming to self-consciousness in the African savannah and the caves of southern France, and still flickering in the psyche of a Connecticut kid? Maybe it's a swath of memory that stretches out behind me into the distant past, like the tail of a comet or the wake of a boat.

Sometimes what I yearn for is not a time in the past but a depth that can be accessed in the present. As I tell myself in a mongrel declaration of my spiritual path, written down and rewritten every few months for the past forty years, "What I long for is always accessible, in the depths, here and now."

As I face the fire tonight, I feel the darkness, chilly, pushing in around me. It hides all the nocturnal dangers my imagination can hatch and real dangers, like bears catching my scent and starting to search for the canister of food I need to wedge under the boulder I saw down the trail a ways. The fire protects me, or at least that's how I imagine it. The smoke is my ally, too. Native peoples on Turtle Island purify spaces by burning sage; I use the smoke to rid the tent site of mosquitoes. The smoke also lifts my thoughts—not quite prayers—up through the hemlock branches to whatever forces might be floating overhead. It perfumes my shirt, planting a reminder that will yank me back to the fire when I place grimy clothes in the washing machine back at home. Smoke traces once held me back from washing a fleece jacket, and for several weeks I savored the scent each time I wore it, back in Boston, on the bridge between smell and memory.

I sit in reverie, watching how flames consume the sticks and how the coals pulsate, as if orange blood were flowing through them. Focused on the fire, savoring the simplicity, I feel content. I also feel the first wave of grogginess, and soon I stop putting fresh branches on the fire. Over the next half hour I flip half-burned sticks to get the unburned ends into the flames. Soon, with all of the fresh wood turning into coals, too, the last flames flicker and die away. As if on cue, a mosquito buzzes up to my ear, nudging me into my nylon shelter for the night.

Around 5:30, dim light and early birds lift me out of sleep. I wake up stiff. The prospect of stuffing damp and dirty gear into the pack and hoisting the load up onto my sore shoulders is enough to make me want to leave everything right where it is, a present for the next backpacker. As I linger in the sleeping bag, my mind starts seeking—and finding—legitimate reasons for giving up the climb that awaits me and hiking straight back out. Luckily, something more awake than I am reminds me to shift from feeling to acting. I say to myself, "What needs to happen next is for me to unzip the bag. Let's do that." Just that single action, like a priest lifting up the chalice in the Eucharist or Sen-no-Rikyū presenting a bowl of tea to a guest. I then writhe my way out of the sleeping bag, pull on the fleece quarter-zip that was serving as my pillow, get into my shorts, pivot to stick my feet out of the bivy, put on my boots, stand up, walk off into the woods, pee, get the bear canister, and start boiling water for coffee and oatmeal. Completion of these simple tasks lifts me out of my morning aches . . . physical and mental. This practice of doing one simple task at a time doesn't always free me from my morning funk, but it does give me some momentum as I start moving through another day.

After eating instant oatmeal with brown sugar, then cleaning the pot and packing everything up, I try to erase my traces and restore the site to a natural state. I hoist the pack back onto my sore hips. As I start to walk away, I stop, turn around, bow to the place, and thank it for being my home for the night. Of my many rituals on the trail, this one feels most rooted in my gut.

While this sort of ritual connects us to what is happening around us right now, many rituals reenact the past. Mircea Eliade wrote about how the religious person, *homo religiosus*, in an effort to get closer to the sacred, ritually reenacts moments when the sacred was present, like the moment of creation, when the world was crackling with the presence of the divine, or when God in the flesh walked among us. We see this type of ritual behavior when Jews position themselves close to God the creator by working six days and taking the seventh off. Or when Christians reenact the Last Supper.

Another way to draw close to the sacred is through reenactment by imitating historical figures who were divine or simply closely connected to a divinity. Pilgrims follow in the footsteps of Christ as they walk the Via Dolorosa. Muslims reenact Hagar's frantic search for water as they run between two hills, now in a long corridor inside the Great Mosque. Buddhists venture to the Mahabodhi temple in Bodhgaya to sit in meditation there like the Buddha did more than 2,500 years ago. On the Shikoku circuit, pilgrims walk in Kūkai's footsteps, though not alone, for they believe that he goes along with them, as reflected in the slogan for the pilgrimage: "going together, two people" (*dōgyō ni'nin*). In this way, pilgrims draw close to Kūkai and perhaps even enter into communion with this saint.

Like seekers on the island of Shikoku or up on Mount Hiei, many pilgrims walk in a loop. In Ireland, pilgrims may venture forth on *turas*, pilgrimages around a circuit with stops at sacred stones, wells, cross pillars, and gravesites of Celtic saints.[72] South Asian religions all maintain the tradition of circumambulating, usually clockwise like the journey of the sun through the sky each day. On Java, pilgrims walk around Borobudur, a temple fashioned as a mandala representing the cosmic mountain Meru and inscribed with scenes from the prototypical Buddhist pilgrimage of the young seeker Sudhana.

Hindu, Buddhist, Jain, and Bon pilgrims circle Mount Kailash in southwestern Tibet. Some Buddhists cover the thirty-two miles by doing prostrations. Moving across a landscape that they construe as a mandala with five "meditation buddhas,"[73] they circle the mountain one body length at a time. Extending out and dropping to the ground, they land on palms covered with leather pads and drop onto the belly, flat, with eight places on their bodies—their knees, stomach, chest, mouth, forehead, and palms—touching the ground. Some observers interpret this as "a complete offering of the self, uniting body with earth in total submission before [Mount] Kailas."[74]

Then the pilgrims stand up, do a triple bow—palms together in front of the forehead, over the mouth, and before the chest—take several steps forward to where their hands just were, and drop down again. In this expression of reverence and humility, it takes twenty days to get all the way around the mountain.

What might a comparable way of hiking entail? Full prostrations the 2,168-mile length of the Appalachian Trail? Take four steps, stop, bow to the woods, drop to the ground, stand up, express thanks, repeat. Or pause every six feet, check in with each of the six senses. Then walk six more feet and repeat.

Circumabulation appears in smaller rituals, too, like the Lakota sun dance, the Hopi snake dance, and the Mesoamerica *volador* ritual, in which four people—representing the four directions as well as earth, air, fire, and water—"fly" in widening circles upside down as the ropes tied to their waists unwind from the top of a thirty-meter pole, while a fifth person remains standing on the top of the pole, dancing and playing a flute. Or the *umrah*: circling the Kaaba seven times at the beginning of the hajj. Hindu pilgrims walk around a sculpture of Shiva's bull Nandi on Chamundi Hill near Mysore. In some Japanese festivals, a portable mikoshi shrine is carried by virile—and often intoxicated—locals on a circuit through the town, thereby affording the kami temporarily enshrined in the mikoshi a chance to bestow blessings door to door.

The circle is a symbol of the cycle of regenerative energy seen in the progression of the seasons, the apparent flight of the sun each day, and the movement of water from sky to earth and back up. The circle also represents wholeness and unity, like cosmic mandalas and the wedding rings slipped onto fingers in one of the holiest of unions. In Zen, the *ensō* calligraphic circle represents awakening, as does another circle, the full moon.

Replete with circular imagery and movements, rituals in many cultures are seen as sustaining certain facets of nature, whether processes like fertility or, by extension, the cosmos itself. We see this in the fire sacrifice in India, which is centered on the creative power of *tapas*, heat, and on the god Agni, a name that shares an Indo-European root with "ignite." In western Japan, as we saw before, pilgrims travel a circuit to thirty-three temples, and through their austerities, prayers, and offerings they keep benefits flowing, thanks to the power of Kannon, the bodhisattva of compassion to whom they pray.

On this trip I will be hiking in a loop, or at least most of it, with the last arc handled by the driver kind enough to pick me up when I hitchhike from the Crawford Path trailhead back to my car. For me, hiking loops is simply a way to avoid doing sections of trail twice. That being said, I do recognize how this and other hikes serve to keep things circulating, at least in and around my body. Blood flows from my heart, out through an intricate system of arteries, and then back through my veins. I drink from my bottle, and the water spreads through my body and passes out into the hydrological cycle. My thoughts pass through my mind and then reappear, like the sun coming around the other side of the earth to rise again in the east. I breathe air into my lungs and then back out. My body releases carbon dioxide to the trees that make oxygen for a later breath.

SIX

Mountains and Other Destinations

> Thousands of tired, nerve-shaken, over-civilized people are beginning to find out that going to the mountains is going home.
>
> —JOHN MUIR[75]

> Climb the mountains and get their good tidings. Nature's peace will flow into you as sunshine flows into trees. The wind will blow their own freshness into you, and the storms their energy, while cares will drop off like autumn leaves.
>
> —JOHN MUIR[76]

AFTER LEAVING THE TENT SITE I hike a hundred yards up the trail, drop steeply down on the Dry River Cutoff, and cross the river. This makes me what Hindus call a *tīrthayātrika*, a wanderer who frequents crossroads and seeks river crossings. From there I gaze up a muddy trail—like a bog tilted forty-five degrees—that extends for two miles to join the Appalachian Trail at the Mizpah Hut. I can feel the lactic acid in my quads, deposited there by my exertions on the hike up the river yesterday. My body wants to go on strike, but I take a deep breath and the first uphill step. I keep my legs moving, and ninety muddy, sweaty minutes later I arrive at the hut.

In the world of hiking and backpacking these days, accolades are getting directed at thru-hikers setting records. With colorful trail names, light packs, and fierce stamina, they pound along the Appa-lachian, Continental Divide, and Pacific Crest trails. The hard-core among them walk up to fifty miles a day. To cover such distances, at first light they break camp—often nothing more than a tarp hung over a sheet that has been sewn into a sleeping pouch—and, before making coffee or eating anything, they log five or ten miles. The ultra-zealous reduce weight to a minimum, drinking water out of a soda bottle to cut half an ounce relative to the bottles sold at REI.

Benton MacKaye proposed the Appalachian Trail in 1920, and over several decades volunteers spliced sections into an unbroken path. The first thru-hiker was WWII veteran Earl Shaffer, who "came to the trail in 1948 trying to escape his depression and the recollection of war's horrors."[77] Thousands of thru-hikers have fol-lowed his lead in the sixty-seven years since.

Glad to be out of the muck and at the top of the Dry River Cut-off, I plant my sweaty self on a rock beside the hut, a stone's throw from where the Appalachian Trail emerges out of the woods, lingers briefly on flat rocks, and turns up a steep slope that seems more like a dry cascade than a trail. As I sit there swigging from my water bot-tle, a twenty-something hiker appears on the A.T., nearly jogging. Seeing his slender frame, light hiking shoes, and GoLite pack, I have a sense he's coming from Georgia, a perception that gets confirmed when I hear him ask a hut attendant, who is outside repairing a win-dow, about thru-hikers who may have slept there last night.

But what strikes me most is how he ignores me when I greet him. Maybe as he approached he saw my traditional leather boots. Or perhaps he deduced from my gray hair and chubbiness that I, unlike him, was not scurrying the 2,168 miles from Springer Mountain in Amicalola Falls State Park down in Georgia all the way up to Mount Katahdin in north-central Maine. Either way, he seems to be a man on a mission. After poking his head into the hut, he gets right back on the trail, hurrying north.

This encounter gets me thinking about how thru-hiking can devolve into get-quickly-thru-this-place hiking as opposed to what I'm advocating here: be-fully-in-this-place hiking. I realize that speedy thru-hikers may cherish the Appalachian Trail and the land through which it passes. They surely have powerful experiences along the way. And if they weren't environmentalists before they started hiking, I imagine they are by the time they get to Maine. But amped-up thru-hiking, or at least the mystique surrounding it, can lead to disdain for other hikers or their gear and feed a competitive approach to being in the woods: How long did this section of the A.T. take *you*? Who has thru-hiked the A.T. the quickest? Who has hiked the Pacific Crest Trail from the Mexican border to Canada and back in one season? Who has walked the length of the Continental Divide Trail in the gnarliest weather or has survived the scariest "epics"? Who has thru-hiked all three trails? In one year?

Granted, some days I push myself on the trail to get to a summit. Or at least to a high spot with views, like the section of the Appalachian Trail that extends across the Connecticut–Massachusetts border from Salisbury into Sheffield, or the Muir Snowfield on the south side of Mount Rainier. Today my goal is Mount Pierce, a modest peak on the ridge that extends from Mount Webster to Mount Jackson, Mount Pierce, Mount Eisenhower, Mount Franklin, Mount Monroe, Lakes of the Clouds, and on up to the summit of Mount Washington. Of course, I'm not alone in being drawn to rocky heights. For most of us, mountains offer a place to step back from the minutiae of life and see the big picture or simply recharge after a stressful time. An early Buddhist recluse wrote,

> With clear waters and massive boulders,
> frequented by monkey and deer,
> covered with moss and water weeds:
> these rocky crags refresh me.[78]

Not that mountains are always a restorative sanctuary. Towering above cultivated fields and forests, beyond the comfort zones of most people, a mountain exudes power with its sheer mass, dizzying cliffs, and sudden onslaughts of thunder and lightning. All of us who venture up the slopes feel that power. Even those who simply gaze up from the valley below confront the bulk of the mountain, towering, unmoving, perhaps threatening. In Exodus the Israelites felt it: "On the morning of the third day there was thunder and lightning, as well as a thick cloud on the mountain, and a blast of a trumpet so loud that all the people who were in the camp trembled" (Exodus 19:16). They and other ancestors would have told us that mountain power is to be respected, regardless of the form it takes, whether sudden avalanches, whiteouts, bears in thickets, rattlesnakes on ledges, demons tricking us, or God speaking though burning bushes and thunderstorms. Early Indians saw mountains as the home of a wild howling deity, Rudra, who is associated with the hunt. Those who gave the name Eiger—German for "ogre"—to that imposing peak in the Alps may have run into a large-headed beast there. With similar dangers in Chinese mountains, pilgrims there have hung mirrors on their backs to ward off goblins.[79] Aware of such threats, Ge Hong (283-343) wrote, "Most of those who are ignorant of the proper method for entering mountains will meet with misfortune and mishap."[80]

Reaching up from bedrock into the clouds, shrouded in mist, with shadowed ravines carved into their flanks, mountains also move us with a sense of majesty and mystery. Encountering this power, Wordsworth, Coleridge, and other Romantics in the nineteenth century devoted gallons of ink to "the sublime," and from there it was a short step to believing that sublime nature is an expression of the divine, and the appreciation of this sublimity is a way to connect with the divine. This notion reverberated through Concord in the writings of the Transcendentalists. As Emerson once put it, "Standing on the bare ground,—my head bathed by the blithe air, and uplifted into infinite space,—all mean egotism vanishes. I become a transparent eye-ball; I am nothing: I see all; the currents of the Universal Being circulate through me; I am part or particle of God."[81]

The Japanese have a rough equivalent to "the sublime": *yūgen*, which can be translated as "subtle profundity." The character *yū* (幽) means "faint," "dim," and "hazy," while *gen* (玄) connotes blackness and mystery. Imagine the faint mountains in East Asian landscape paintings, appearing through the mist or perhaps receding back into it.

Mountains take on an array of other meanings. To the Chinese, mountains generate the qi that circulates through the world, and for this reason they are seen as "dispersing life" (散生) to the myriad things in nature.[82] Arne Naess, climber and doyen of Deep Ecology, highlights the "symbolic values" of mountains: the upward movement of the eye and the climber, representing "increase of any positive kind"; height, symbolizing "excellence, nobility, majesty, steadiness, coolness, superiority"; transcendence of the ordinary human condition; closeness to heaven; the struggle of climbers analogous to the struggle "towards the highest quality"; the unattainability of certain summits, akin to the unattainability of the absolute.[83]

Carrying this symbolic freight, mountains are the feature in the landscape that religions typically imbue with the most sacred power. Jutting up into the heavens, drawing close to the gods or God, mountains are where humans can best access ultimate powers. To the religious seeker, mountains are the place to feel Rudolf Otto's *mysterium tremendum*. Like Jesus, Buddha is known for ascending mounts to give sermons, including Vulture Peak in northern India, where he purportedly delivered such foundational scriptures of Mahāyāna Buddhism as the Lotus Sutra and the "wisdom sutras."

The thru-hiker scurries on his way, up the steep rocky section behind me. A minute later I leave the flat area next to the hut and start following him. After climbing several hundred feet and getting the sweat flowing again, I traverse at tree line to the top of Mount Pierce. My efforts reward me with a view of the Crawford Path snaking its way along the ridge to Mount Washington, what the Abenaki have called Agiocochook, "home of the Great Spirit." Five miles away, the mountain stands massive, holding court as it looms over northern New Hampshire and western Maine.

Towering peaks like Washington are sometimes seen as the axis mundi, the center of the world around which everything revolves and up which humans gain access to the heavens or, as in China, down which they connect to the underworld. The Lakota see Mount Harney in the Black Hills as the center of their world. In some cultures the axis mundi is a sacred pole or pillar, or a structure like the Kaaba or St. Peter's Basilica with its towering dome, but for Buddhism—and Hinduism—it is indeed a mountain, if a mythological one: Mount Meru, or Sumeru, rising tens of thousands of miles into the heavens and surrounded by seven concentric rings of mountains and a vast sea with four continents, the southern one of which, Jambudvīpa, "Rose-Apple Island," is South Asia, the known world when this cosmology was conceived. Containing all of this is an eighth ring of mountains, composed of solid iron. As the axis mundi, Meru is equated with our bodily axis, the spinal cord, and the various levels of reality that are mapped onto and above the mountain analogized to the hierarchy of energy centers or chakras along the spinal cord.

Hindus and Buddhists see Mount Kailash in western Tibet as the earthly manifestation of Meru. They draw correspondences between the distinctive bands of rock on the face of the peak and levels of reality. They view the mountain as a whole, a bit inaccurately, as the source of the four great rivers of the Indian subcontinent: the Indus, the Brahmaputra, the Karnali, and the Sutlej. Legend has it that when the great ascetic Milarepa competed with a magician of the indigenous Bon religion for control of the peak, the magician tumbled down from the summit, and as he fell, his shamanic drum gouged the south face of the mountain into a pattern that believers see as the *svastika*, the ancient Aryan symbol of good fortune that Hitler appropriated for his own purposes. Tibetan Buddhists now regard Kailash as the domain of Demchog, the Tibetan equivalent of the Hindu god Shiva.

In the Chinese worldview, mountains are "uncultivated, untamed, and primordial," and as a realm of the unknown, mountain landscapes are replete with "the intrinsic numinosity of nature found in peaks, cliffs, vistas, caves, grottoes, springs, rocks, or trees."[84] They are the preferred dwelling place of hermits, some of whom have been regarded as "immortals." Sacred Buddhist mountains are the abode of bodhisattvas, like Samantabhadra on Mount Emei. Chinese mountains have drawn pilgrims wanting to "seek a vision of the deity, perform a penance, ask for heirs or cures, or pray for good health and long life for themselves and their family members."[85]

Sacred mountains also cover the volcanic archipelago that is Japan. South of Mount Hiei, in the center of the Kii Peninsula, is Mount Kōya, one of the sacred peaks associated with Kūkai. Up in northern Japan is Mount Osore, where blind shamanesses convey messages from the dead. As part of the assimilation of Buddhism that started in the sixth century, indigenous kami—often seen as dwelling in the mountains—were equated with foreign buddhas or bodhisattvas, and some thinkers mapped the mountains of Japan in Buddhist terms. Onto the twin peaks of Futagoyama on the Kunisaki Peninsula in Kyūshū, Buddhists superimposed the Lotus Sutra. The text's twenty-eight chapters were linked to twenty-eight temples in valleys on the sides of the mountain, and each of the 69,380 characters in the Chinese rendering of the scripture was represented by a Buddhist statue. "Thus," Allan Grapard tells us, "reading the scripture one discovered the mountain; walking on the mountain became the equivalent of reading the scripture: the mountain was textualized, and the text was, if this term can be coined, *enmountained*."[86] Similarly, as we have seen, yamabushi steeped in the Tendai and Shingon branches of Buddhism have mapped the mountainous landscape around Mount Ōmine with the Diamond and Womb mandalas.

Mountains are so central to Zen's monastic and symbolic universes that major temples are often referred to as mountains, as in the "five mountain" system of designating important Zen temples in China and Japan. Their gardens, though originally not as "Zen" as modern writers have made them out to be, are often rendered in a style called *karesansui* (枯山水), "old withered [trees,] mountains and waters." An expression for setting out on the Zen spiritual path is "entering a mountain," with the character for "mountain" connoting both the steep location and the monastery located there. To build a monastery is referred to as "opening a mountain," which necessitates taming the beings that have lived in that place, whether wild animals, demons, or ghosts.[87] Not that all inhabitants of the mountains were tamed: "Recluses were the personification of the mountains themselves: lonely, untamed, unkempt—storehouses of the secrets of nature. Caves, huts, and mountain temples were their lairs. From ancient times, the mysterious recluses had mysterious powers."[88]

In some Shintō rituals, conical sand "mountains" a few feet high are sculpted to provide a landing place and temporary residence for a kami called down by prayers and offerings. In the Gion Festival every July in Kyoto, the smaller festival carts that carry kami and are pulled along the parade route by college students looking to earn a few thousand yen are called *yama*, mountains. In Shintō, actual mountains are the realm of a colorful legion of kami, spirits, demons, shapeshifters like foxes, and ghosts of the deceased. During winter, the higher elevations of Japan are the abode of the mountain gods. As the weather gets warmer, these kami descend to valleys to serve as paddy gods, whose job it is to watch over the rice. Festivals at the time of planting welcome and entertain them in the spring, while harvest festivals thank them and send them back up the mountain in the fall.

To get to mountains, we usually have to travel away from human habitation and head to the backcountry, to the "interior." The Japanese term for this is *oku*, a term that appears in haiku poet Bashō's travel diary, *Oku no hosomichi*, "the narrow path to the interior." Mountain temples may have their own *oku*, their own inner sanctum. An example of this is the Oku-no-in on Mount Kōya, the building where the Shingon Buddhist faithful believe Kūkai has been dwelling in a deep state of meditation for the past 1,200 years.

When we leave the tamed nature of parks and farms, we can engage in what the Chinese call "mountain wandering." While ambling along mountain trails, we may even intuit the presence of the yamabushi's guardian Fudō, which literally means "not moving," at least in the sense of not being rattled by the things that affect the rest of us, such as the mental hindrances that he lassos with the rope he holds in one hand and then slays with the sword he wields in the other. If we're lucky, we may come to intuit the immovable in ourselves. This imperturbability may take the form of the voice that motivates us to keep walking when blisters get insistent. Or the sky mind that quietly takes in the Yosemite panorama from Glacier Point.

With their power and proximity to the divine, mountains have been the destination of pilgrims seeking an optimal place for religious practice. Caves in the Himalayas, hermitages for "forest-dwelling" monks in the highlands of Thailand, and Dionysiou Monastery on Mount Athos have all drawn mystics. Mahakashyapa, one of the Buddha's disciples, purportedly wrote,

Fair uplands rain-refreshed, and resonant
With crested creatures' cries antiphonal,
Lone heights where silent rishis oft resort:
Those are the hills wherein my soul delights.[89]

Zen visionaries have even viewed mountains as teachers and role models. In his *Sansuikyō* (Mountains and Waters Sūtra), Dōgen writes that the "mountains and waters are presenting the Way of ancient buddhas" and "each one, abiding in its own state of being, actualizes far-reaching virtues."[90] Each mountain and stream, is perfect just as it is and showing us how to be.

Across history, religious virtuosi have had foundational religious experiences in the heights. Muhammad received his first revelation from Allah while spending a night in the hills above Mecca. Milarepa had visions in a cave tucked in the Himalayas. Moses was called by God on the flank of Mount Horeb. Later, through thunder and lightning, he and the rest of the Israelites received the ten utterances there, early on in their forty years of wandering in the wilds of the Sinai Peninsula.

Of course, the allure of mountains extends beyond religious seekers. Lots of us head to the hills in search of excitement, not tranquility. This comes, of course, with pitfalls. Those who see mountains as an amphetamine for rushes can stumble into attachment to a goal—"We have to summit or else!"—or attachment to the "epic" drama of pursuing that goal. To climb with this drivenness is to set oneself up for agitation if not injury.

Summit fever is not the only form of agitation on the trail. Some days worries come along for the hike and spend the day buzzing in my head, refusing to stay back in the car. Or something prods me to push the limits of my endurance. This can set me up for frustration with a companion's slower pace or with the pain that grows through the day as my right femur slams again and again into the back of my patella. My ego sometimes latches on to the distance to be hiked or the number of miles to the turn-around point, as I "do" a section of trail. What am I trying to attain—or purge—in such goal-oriented exertion? What manic energy am I trying to burn out of my system? On days when I hike with urgency, "doing battle" with the incline and slick rocks, my ego can get inflated by its conquest of the terrain. This is one reason why warrior rhetoric about spiritual paths makes me nervous.

The agitation that drives people toward summits can take other forms. For some people, hiking, like cross-fit workouts and obstacle courses, cultivates and expresses toughness. With the trail as our stage, we may try to impress others with our position on the stronger and savvier end of the hiking spectrum. A bit aloof, and self-aggrandizing. Upon our return we may slip "gnarly" into our descriptions of the hike. This sort of intensity can permeate other areas of our lives, where we push hard—*doing, doing, doing*—and render ourselves frenetic. What motivates this? Fear of getting stuck in a boring life? Fear of being left behind? Fear of being out of it, whatever the "it" might be? Fear of death? As Pascal once put it, a pauper with lots of distractions is happier than a king with nothing to do.

My knees and psyche prefer a less intense way of hiking. They want me to practice what I preach and make sure my hike isn't some test of strength and stamina but rather the simple act of being fully in a place. That, not a summit, is my goal. To go slow, feel my aching body, and pay attention to what I'm seeing, smelling, and hearing. I may not get more than a mile up the path. I may spend most of the day just sitting on one rock, or gazing at a single sight. Ideally, my focus is not on how close I'm getting to my destination up the trail but on how close I'm getting to what's around me. It's about tapping in, not topping off.

So when I manage to approach an outing as a way to serve my spirit rather than my ego, I'm not striving to reach a summit. Insofar as

I may have a geographical goal on the hike, it's an exceptional place to meditate, and when backpacking, a beautiful spot to roll out my sleeping bag. The site may lie only three or four miles up the trail. I may spend much of the day there. I may linger through the morning rather than carbo-load quickly with oatmeal and bound up the trail to click off some early-morning miles.

This approach accords well with my sixty-year-old body. As I walk slowly along the Appalachian Trail on the sloping crest of Mount Pierce, I feel myself expanding with the view, and at the same time I start doubting the ability of my knees to support me. Will one of them snap or crumple, sending me crashing down and rendering me unable to hike out? Like many of its cousins throughout the White Mountains, my route since the hut has been a jumbled staircase of rocks with few switchbacks. When I got home after a recent hike, I referred to the range as "a pile of rocks with a couple of trees." Non-technical hiking in the Rockies and Cascades, even in higher elevations, is easier on arthritic joints, for the maintained trails there more likely consist of switchbacks with smoother surfaces. Insofar as I stick to trails, I'd rather hike twenty miles with a 4,000-foot elevation gain in the Cascades than ten miles with a 2,000-foot gain in the Whites.

By directing our attention to *how* we hike as opposed to *where* we're headed, and taking as our goal sitting quietly in a beautiful spot rather than summiting a gnarly peak, we can begin to shift from ego-driven *doing* mode to spirit-filled *being* mode, from proving something in nature to exploring how we *are* nature. In this way we can complement views out across the landscape with views of what's going on inside.

This is, of course, a way of pilgrimage that steers clear of trying to get to the *1000 Places to See before You Die*, an approach that slips into checklist consumer tourism with a hefty carbon price tag, not to mention the stress of scurrying around the globe in cramped airplanes. Granted, traveling to appreciate amazing places and in the process becoming more inclined to protect them are preferable to flying to Scotland simply for a round of golf and a shot of Glenfiddich. But the path is about how to *be* in a place, any place, fully present in and *as* nature.

SEVEN

Vistas and Visions

KENSHŌ —
"SEEING INTO
[ONE'S] NATURE"

The expansive sky does not obstruct
the floating white clouds.
—SEKITŌ[91]

Heaven and earth have the same root,
myriad things are one body.
—SENGZHAO[92]

I came to realize clearly, that mind is no other than
mountains and rivers and the great earth.
—DŌGEN[93]

I PAUSE AT THE JUNCTION where the Crawford Path joins the Appalachian Trail after winding up along Gibbs Creek from the Notch. Straight ahead, Mount Washington presents itself to me, massive and unmoving.

Many of us hike for views like this, regardless of whether we summit. We seek grand vistas—and photographs of them—as a reward for our pilgrimages into nature. Anticipating the view, we may feel excitement as we start to emerge above tree line. When we step out of the trees and look out over the krummholz, our spirits get lifted by the expanse, or we feel disappointed to find the peak shrouded in fog.

Out on the trail, however, some of the most powerful visions are not across a rugged landscape, and to experience them we don't need to reach a summit or possess youthful courage (or risky stupidity). Nor do we have to drive—or fly—long distances to trailheads. These visions can be achieved closer to home. If Emerson's Oversoul permeates all things, qi moves through all of nature, and kami are scattered across the landscape (or, better yet, life-scape), can I sense these facts in the old oak lording over the saplings in the woods on Palfrey Hill above my semi-urban neighborhood? Do I need to climb remote mountains to trigger the *mysterium tremendum*? As a boy the Buddha got a foretaste of enlightenment while sitting under a rose apple tree watching his father plow a field. Later in life his great awakening happened on the edge of a village, not up in a cave on the side of a Himalayan peak (even though Zen artists portray him as "descending the mountain" after his enlightenment experience). His preferred lecture hall was not a backcountry tent site or base camp beside a glacier but a manicured garden.

Simply put, remote wilderness is not required for religious experiences. The rocky spot where Allah spoke to Muhammad overlooked the crossroad markets of Mecca. Bernadette was out collecting firewood with two other girls on the edge of Lourdes when she saw the lady in white. Buddha was sitting under a tree near a village in northern India when he broke free from suffering. St. Francis was in the chapel of San Damiano near Assisi when he saw Christ, and Julian had her visions while mortared off in a cell on the outside wall of the cathedral in Norwich.

But impactful encounters and visions, whether in the wild or on the edge of human habitation, are not the last word in transformative experiences. Subtler vistas open up all the time on the trail. The approach to hiking I've been sketching here helps us cultivate a way of paying attention, of *being* in the woods, that diverges from the desire to prove something or add a summit to our list of exploits. It's about emptying ourselves of our drivenness and simply giving our attention to the act of walking and the place through which we move. Though we get sweaty, dirty, and covered with DEET, we are cleansing ourselves internally, and this, in turn, clears our sight.

The process of mental quieting may take a while. Few of us can set foot onto a trail and immediately stop thinking about things back home. Worries tag along, like lampreys on the side of a shark. But gravity helps. Pack straps wedge into our trapezius muscles. Knees start to ache. Sweat runs down our forehead. Not unlike seated meditation, hiking compels us to enter the raw physicality of what we're doing. True, we may start obsessing about a blister on a heel or soreness in a knee, but we keep walking. Step, step, bug, step, wipe sweat, step, stub toe on rock, step again, stiff quad, step, shoulder strap, step, thirst, step, step. A mile or two up the trail, pack straps adjusted, muscles warmed up, a rhythm usually sets in. Our breath settles. Barring severe pain or resistance to being out on the hike in the first place, our mouths quiet down. As—or if—we stop talking with others in our group, our inner chatter dissipates, too. We start to attend more to the roots undulating across the trail and the way the sun hits our forehead. Challenges along the path sharpen our attention—a boulder to scamper over, mud to step around, a stream to cross on slick rocks. In this way the quality of our focus shifts, from fixating on thoughts and worries to paying attention to what's happening around us.

Basically, our mind is getting emptied. What may open up is a calm, attentive awareness, free from obsessive thinking and worrying. And when thoughts do arise, they pass through us like how a cloud, a bird, or a falling star passes through the sky. We can call this awareness "empty-sky mind." In Japanese, the character for "emptiness" is also the character for "sky" (空),[94] and Buddhism is replete with metaphors about clouds drifting unimpeded across a vast blue sky.

Zen sometimes refers to this sky mind as "no mind" (*mushin*), an awareness that is there in the background while our thinking scurries about, latching on to things, like a monkey in a fruit tree. Shunryu Suzuki called it big mind, transcending our small mind of analyzing, judging, and worrying. Others have termed it mirror mind, insofar as it perceives things clearly and doesn't react.

As backpackers know, when spending extended time in the wilderness, our minds get progressively emptied and this big sky mind opens up. With our normal frenetic consciousness quieted down, we pay better attention—without even "efforting" to do so. We notice things more vividly. Tiny heather flowers. Yucca jutting out on the lower slopes of San Gorgonio. The insistent drumming of a red-bellied woodpecker on Stratton Mountain. A pile of grizzly shit east of Athabasca. The buzz of the cicada starts to pierce us, like it did to Bashō on his trail:

> Silence.
> The buzz of the cicadas
> penetrates the rocks.

In one respect, when our minds get emptied, we get filled by whatever we experience. As Dōgen famously put it, "To learn the self is to forget the self; to forget the self is to be confirmed by the ten-thousand things." There is no felt sense of being apart from the sunset, the sound of a warbler, the smell of mud emerging through the spring thaw. Though it usually lasts only for a moment and no words can capture it, we might be inclined to exclaim, "In that moment, I was the sunset and the sunset was me." This experience is what Dōgen calls "the dropping off of mind and body."

In more philosophical terms, it is the dissolution of the separation between ourselves and what we experience, between subject and object. In such moments it is not me and the blazing sky, me and the call of the songbird, but just the sunset, just the birdcall. Though the experience may be mediated at a preconscious level by concepts, in that moment of experience there is no sense of "me" apart from any of those things, but simply the raw, immediate experience. It is no longer the case that we are *having* an experience *of* those things but we *are* the experience, we are those things as they happen in the moment. As Thich Nhat Hanh puts it, "If you are a mountain climber or someone who enjoys the countryside, or the green forest, you know that the forests are our lungs outside of our bodies. . . . We should be able to be our true self. That means we should be able to be the river, we should be able to be the forest. . . . That is the non-dualistic way of seeing."[95]

We may even realize that we are part of the interconnected web of life, that "I" am nature doing its thing through me, as me. I am one temporary configuration in the field of energy called nature. To shift metaphors, I am a wave in a vast ocean of energy, and while on retreat in the woods, I may realize that I am inseparable from that unified expanse of water, even as I take my particular form as one wave, one upwelling of that whole. Though I normally think of myself as a separate entity, as an autonomous wave, I am actually a water-as-wave wave. I am *me*—but not me in the way I think of myself in normal egocentricity. We discern nonduality: not two and not one. Not two: I am not apart from the unified field of energy. Not one: I am not fused with it in a way that erases my particularity. In terms of the famous line in the Heart Sutra, "form is emptiness": I realize the ocean of energy of which I am part. And "emptiness is form": that ocean exists only as formed waves, as particular forms like me.

On the trail, as our minds get emptied and our senses get tuned—perhaps with a good dose of endorphins—we also start to see things more clearly. With our analytical mind quieted, no longer reaching out to things and in effect grabbing on to them, things come to us. With our minds like a mirror rather than a hook, things appear to us, doing their thing, "self-so," in what Buddhists call their "suchness." In Dōgen's parlance, we experience *genjō kōan*: the immediate presencing of each thing. In its exuberant flowering, leafing, gurgling, scatting, or chirping, each thing is manifesting itself in its distinctiveness. Mount Rainier rises up above the wildflowers in Spray Park. A leopard slug leaves a veneer of slime along a wet nurse log. A dry canyonland of bark extends up along the trunk of a Douglas fir. Here in the Whites, alpine heather reaches out with delicate mauve flowers.

To experience things fully as they present themselves in their suchness is not to see them as symbolizing something. Granted, Japanese Buddhist poetry is replete with associations between pine trees and longevity, bamboo and flexibility, cherry blossoms and transient beauty. But Dōgen is trying to lead us out of thinking and into direct contact with the raw givenness of things. Hemlock branches weighed down with globs of snow, dripping in the afternoon sun. Petals of silver light flickering on lake ripples. The underbellies of poplar leaves fluttering in the breeze. And we do not feel separate.

Walking in nature thus gives us a different sense of self. The Australian environmental activist John Seed once said, "I am that part of the rain forest recently emerged into thinking." Today on the trail I am nature doing its thing in me, through me, as me.

When you hike, or stroll down the block, see if you can *be* nature, not just walk through it. Feel yourself as a mammal, moving your legs like deer and bears do. Imagine yourself as part of that swirling ocean of energy that is nature, and then, like every mountain, tree, squirrel, and stream, feel yourself moving in the interconnected system, the eternal dance, that is unfolding here. Feel yourself as a configuration of energy, distinct yet connected to everything around you.

If we cultivate these modes of awareness, we can better savor the unique and precious things we encounter on the trail: Our bodies breathing and sweating. This chipmunk scooting in and out of the tumble of rocks next to the trail on Mount Pierce, hoping for a nut from my trail mix. The thunderhead forming above Bott Spur.

Relishing each element of nature, we practice what tea ceremony practitioners term *ichigo ichi'e,* "one moment, one encounter." Each moment is totally unique, spawned by countless causes and effects. This is it! It happens only once. Right here, right now. A hawk catches an updraft over the ridge, doing its hawk thing in full majesty. A groggy student taps out a text message and spills some coffee as she enters my classroom. Our neighbor's cat Jet flops on her side in our garden, coaxing a scratch.

Woven into all of this is the fact of impermanence. Granted, mountains do persist, which makes them symbols of permanence. But to see with an eye that recognizes the impermanence of everything is to know that Mount Washington will someday erode into a bump and to appreciate the cumulus clouds above Pinkham Notch today, with their own misty cliffs and ravines, no less spectacular than any of the Presidentials laid out beneath them. It's just that granite mountains last a bit longer.

So how can we live in both human time and geological time? Dew vanishes by noon, and Mount Katahdin is a monadnock, a remnant of the massive mountain that encompassed it and eroded away. Mount Everest rises five millimeters a year as tectonic plates keep colliding, but someday it, too, will be reduced to a monadnock, five miles lower than it is now. Blue mountains are indeed constantly walking.

As we hike among mountains, our consciousness is changing as well. Today, my mind shifts abruptly when I step onto the barren summit of Mount Pierce and, suddenly, see the rugged expanse of the Presidentials opened out before me, with the Crawford Path stretching like a rope to the summit cone of Mount Washington. Crawling out on a ledge or popping up above the tree line, we may suddenly receive such a view. In the moment the vista opens up, our consciousness does, too. The mild headache and aching quads were worth it. The exertion has paid off, and we are now rewarded.

About twenty years ago, halfway up the Muir Snowfield on the south side of Mount Rainier, I looked over my shoulder and saw Mount Saint Helens and Mount Hood to the south. My attention got yanked away from the pain that had invaded my knee on the way up from Paradise Lodge. My obsessing about how far it was to Camp Muir dissolved into a macro-view of the Cascades, stretching down into Oregon, under a cloudless sky. On another trip, as the trail approached the Tengboche Monastery, I caught my first glimpse of Ama Dablam, and in that instant my mind expanded up and out to that spectacular mountain.

For pilgrims to Jerusalem, the sudden shift of consciousness may happen in the moment they see the hill that Jews call the Temple Mount and Muslims call Haram al-Sharif, the Noble Sanctuary. For Christians, it may be the moment of seeing Golgotha, "skull hill," inside the Church of the Holy Sepulchre. For others, it might be the first sighting of Mount Shasta, Kilimanjaro, Adam's Peak, Mount Putou, Croagh Patrick, or Mount Tabor. We can only imagine what ancient Greeks felt when they first saw Mount Olympus, when Zoroastrians beheld Hara Berezaiti, or when Daoists trekking across the Taklamakan Desert first spotted the Kun Lun Mountains, abode of the Jade Queen of the West and her peach trees of immortality.

Shifts in consciousness, however, are not always so sudden and powerful. Shunryu Suzuki taught that the fruits yielded by his style of meditation are not religious experiences with thunder, lightning, angels, and white light but something more akin to running your hand through your hair while on a walk in the fog and suddenly realizing that the top of your head has gotten wet.

On some hikes, our consciousness doesn't shift much at all. We may be lost in thought or feeling impatient. The desire to take a photo, eat a quick lunch, and get back down to the chips in the car has more than once seduced me into hurrying. Today I start day-dreaming about the Chinese food that awaits me on my way out of the mountains in Lincoln. In such moments, as in zazen, we remember—yes, mindfulness of a sort—to bring our attention back to the breath and back to the pebbles at our feet.

Heather tendrils cascade onto the trail. The sun burns the top corners of my forehead where my hairline has receded.

The core practice of my hiking is not seeking dramatic views or stepping on summits (and then talking about what mountains I have "done") but, as I said before, bringing my attention back to my body each step of the way, to the little vistas always there around me. Like Buddhists, Iris Murdoch says that in order to love the world we have to see "the world as it is." Simone Weil even tells us that "absolute attention is prayer." To John Muir, this sustained attention to what we encounter on the trail may even result in communion if not union with nature when "you lose consciousness of your separate existence: you blend with the landscape, and become part and parcel of nature."[96] But we should not get stuck in that oneness—nonduality is both not-two and not-one. We have to emerge from that "blending" and embrace our particular body as it walks along. As David Barnhill puts it, "The ideal . . . is not an amorphous oneness with nature but a perceptive and particularized harmony with one's own local area."[97]

Out of that intimacy we may, like Aldo Leopold, come to think like a mountain. We may even feel motivated to protect the peaks and valleys on which we walk, as if they were part of us. Dōgen declares, "Although we say that mountains belong to the country, actually they belong to those who love them. When the mountains love their owners, the wise and virtuous inevitably enter the mountains. And when sages and wise people live in the mountains, because the mountains belong to them, trees and rocks flourish and abound, and the birds and beasts take on a supernatural excellence. This is because the sages and wise people have covered them with their virtue. We should realize that the mountains actually take delight in wise people, actually take delight in sages."[98]

In return, we may take delight in the mountains and woods, with all of their power and mystery. Perhaps we can glimpse the perspective of the Pit River Indians, about whom Jaime de Angulo writes, "To them, the essence of religion is the spirit of wonder, the recognition of life as power, as a mysterious, concentrated form of nonmaterial energy, of something loose about the world and contained in a more or less condensed degree by every object."[99]

Sometimes the most powerful visions are not of grand scenery or the sublime but of ourselves, of our bodies in nature and the wild regions of our mind. John Muir once wrote, "I only went out for a walk, and finally concluded to stay out till sundown, for going out, I found, was really going in."[100] For millennia, mystics have trekked along the mountains and rivers of the mind, and though the inner peaks may be the most formidable, to explore them we do not need to be young, fit, and endowed with enough time and cash to catch a flight to Kathmandu. Anyone can go on this expedition, and perhaps the older pilgrim, free from the hormones and adrenaline of youth, can reach inner destinations more readily.

EIGHT

Beauty and Blazes on the Trail

美と善

BI TO ZEN —
"BEAUTY AND THE GOOD"

> We only value what we know and love, and we no longer know
> or love the wild. So instead we accept substitutes, imitations,
> semblances, fakes—a diminished wild.
>
> —JACK TURNER[101]

I LINGER AT THE JUNCTION, not wanting to part from the view of Mount Washington and not wanting to find out how badly the descent down Crawford Path is going to hammer my knees. Four people—two couples?—in their late teens or early twenties walk up the path, talking loudly. The face of the woman in shorts and tank top is flushed red, which prompts me to wrack my slightly dehydrated brain to remember how the symptoms for heat exhaustion and heatstroke differ. Then I remember that in both cases the person is pale. But she does look wiped out, and the only liquid she's carrying is the dregs in a twenty-ounce bottle of Diet Coke. When she reaches the junction, about ten feet from where I'm standing, one of her companions pulls out a pack of Marlboros and lights up.

We can seek any number of boons when we walk into the woods, and not just a cigarette at our chosen summit for the day. Many hikers hit the trail to get exercise or gain distance from something that's bothering them. Some crave the sense of accomplishment that comes from climbing a peak or walking a great distance. Still others seek invigoration through contact with nature. And for some of us, whether we take a camera, sketchbook, or keen pair of eyes, the main attraction is beauty.

Walkers attuned to beauty, whether along the trail or in a park, can readily appreciate the seven characteristics of Zen art that were lifted up by lay master Shin'ichi Hisamatsu (1889–1980).[102] The first is asymmetry (*fukinsei*), seen in things that are crooked or imbalanced. National-treasure tea bowls droop and bulge, like the off-center rejects I created in a college ceramics class and wrapped in December for the one relative who still smoked. Asymmetry appears in bent and gnarled trees, like the scrub spruce at tree line here on Mount Pierce or the bristlecone pines in the White Mountains of California, conveying naturalness far better than any "perfect" tree getting farmed to hold up tinsel and ornaments. Asymmetry is there in the boulder-strewn rapids of the Kaligandaki, twisting its way down through gorges to the Gangetic plain.

To Hisamatsu, asymmetry connotes "no rule" (*muhō*). Given the forms and formality of Zen, we might find this surprising, though Hisamatsu would argue that monastic rules lead practitioners beyond all rules, or at least beyond attachment to received forms. Accomplished climbers have mastered the basic moves and can now improvise and give the techniques a personal expression, even if appearing off balance or contorted.

As Daoists have argued in their debates with Confucians, nature exhibits patterns far subtler than being straight, upright, and "playing by the rules." Nature's way of ordering itself isn't necessarily symmetrical or linear. It isn't something played out in a geometry of predictability. (I defer to others on fractals, however.) Nature can be unruly. It is often chaotic, ferocious. Here on Crawford Path, I try to imagine how fierce the conditions were in June 1900 when William Curtis and Allan Ormsbee trudged along this ridge and died on the summit cone of Washington.

The second characteristic of Zen art is *kanso*, simplicity, and it permeates Zen life, whether in the stripped-down austerity of the meditation hall or the minimal possessions of the novice. All excess is removed, and colors get subdued. *Kanso* also connotes "freedom from stuff," and it connects to *karumi*, a light touch, not being "heavy-handed." It's there when we open our hands to let nature do its thing, without trying to grab it or making a fist to pound it into submission. To Hisamatsu, *kanso* corresponds to *muzō*, "no complexity." No clutter, just a simple space for a calm, clear mind. And in terms of time, no frenetic scurrying, no rat race. As I am doing here on the north side of Mount Pierce, we slow things down so we can feel our breath, notice each smell and sound as we walk, and be aware of the beautyscape through which we walk.

The third characteristic is *kokō*, literally, "lofty dryness," which Hisamatsu's translator rendered as "sublime austerity." We see this in the weathered siding of old barns in Vermont, or a solitary spruce, stunted and bent by the onshore winds pounding Big Sur. It's here today in the hardy granite humps that rise a foot or two out of the heather. Hisamatsu links this to *mu'i*, "no rank." Things with this characteristic are outside normal aesthetic and social hierarchies, one of a kind, with their own quirky nobility. This compound comprises half of Linji's expression, "true person of no rank." About this "person," Hisamatsu writes, "Since it is without rank, it never gets caught up in anything. It is free, emancipated, or, in more dynamic terms, a free and unhindered functioning."[103]

The fourth characteristic of Zen aesthetics is *jinen*, naturalness. *Jinen* is the Buddhist pronunciation of the compound "*shizen*," which, as we saw before, literally means "in the manner of itself" and refers to how things express their natures spontaneously, without effort. Hisamatsu equates this concept with *mushin*, "no mind": no ego, no self-serving deliberation, no shtick. Zen practitioners and hikers discover jinen and mushin as the calm strength that emerges from being firmly planted wherever one sits or steps. Ideally, we are straightforward, free from trickiness. This slides over into the broader Japanese virtue of sincerity, something I bumped into early on in my time in Japan, when I realized that ending a conversation with typically American throwaway lines like "Let's get together again soon" or "I'll give you a ring" sets up expectations and strikes Japanese as insincere when not followed up with a phone call.

For the fifth characteristic, Hisamatsu lifts up *yūgen*, which he glosses as "profundity, darkness, reverberation, Deep Reserve."[104] He describes this as "a darkness full of calm, a darkness that leads to composure," seen, for example, inside a teahouse,[105] or in mountains shrouded in mist. Things with yūgen are bottomless (*mutei*). We can intuit such depth in nature—and the mind—as we walk through a forest at night or lose ourselves in the pulsating embers of a campfire.

The sixth characteristic is *datsuzoku*, freedom from attachment. Hisamatsu expounds on this in terms of the "Formless Self": "Only the self that, while in the midst of the world, is yet unattached to and free from it is capable of being unrestricted and free in dealing with it. So long as we remain 'something,' we can never be free. Thus, by being nonattached is meant the freedom to take on any form because of not having any form."[106] This is the "free and easy wandering" of Daoist sages. It is *muge*, "no hindrance," a term that appears in the vision of the Flower Garland Sūtra with its notion of "no hindrance between thing and thing." Last week shafts of saffron light pierced a cloudbank as a lone Canada goose, its wings making the sound of a bellows, flew over the house on its way from the Charles River to the high school track and a safe place to spend the night.

Hisamatsu's seventh characteristic is *seijaku*, tranquility, the state of not stirring or not moving (*mudō*), exemplified by Muqi's masterpiece of a black bird sitting alone on a pine branch. Through zazen or some other means, we quiet our minds. Then we maintain this composure in our actions—washing out cereal bowls, driving to work, walking from the parking lot into the office. As a Zen expression puts it, "stillness in moving, moving in stillness." As I walk past the two couples here on the A.T., I bear mute witness to their joking about getting lost. (With no bootleg trails here to seduce them, this is not a likely possibility.)

Hisamatsu's list doesn't exhaust Japan's aesthetic lexicon. When talking about their artistic traditions, Japanese deploy a bevy of other terms. They celebrate *mono no aware*, the "sorrow-tinged appreciation of transient beauty."[107] When a poem or painting leaves them with "lingering emotions," they speak of *yojō*.

But what one hears most in popular discourse about Japanese art are the words *wabi* and *sabi*. Like other aesthetic terms, these two are often vague in the minds of their champions and shrouded in cultural nationalism, as reflected in claims like "These concepts derive from a unique aesthetic sense, and you really have to be born Japanese to get a handle on them." Though aesthetes often conflate these words, as if joined by a hyphen to form a single construct, *wabi-sabi*, we can tease out strands of meaning to distinguish them.

The term *wabi* is the root of the verb, *wabu*, "to languish," from which we get the adjective *wabishii*, rendered in the Kenkyūsha dictionary as "wretched, desolate, forlorn, wintry." It defines *wabi* as "taste for the simple and quiet."[108] Perhaps wabi can best be understood as the beauty seen in rustic simplicity. A rough-hewn cabin, freshly pulled carrots in a cracked earthenware bowl, logs crackling in a fieldstone fireplace.

The companion term *sabi* signifies a kind of simple beauty as well. It is the root of the adjective *sabishii*, "solitary or lonely." It is also a homophone of the character for "rust" or "patina." The *Kenkyūsha* renders *sabi* as "patina; an antique look," and "elegant simplicity." Others portray it as an aesthetic of "old age, loneliness, resignation, and tranquility."[109] Simply put, as an aesthetic category, sabi refers to the aged, dry, weathered look—the patina—of certain things, especially those that are solitary, austere, and tranquil. Sabi is what we see in a cedar snag protruding in the Olympic rainforest or green lichen on chunks of granite here on Mount Pierce. It's there in the weathered barn that Andrew Wyeth painted in *Christina's World*.

In terms of the compound, *wabi-sabi*, think of the lone cypress tree that appears in Big Sur calendars; wabi is there in the hints of something ancient in the twists of the trunk and the cracked rock beneath it, while sabi is found in its solitariness and its dry, wind-beaten texture. At the Lakes of the Clouds Hut below the summit crown of Mount Washington, two miles from where I'm standing, wabi is there in the kitchen's dented pots and rough wood counters, while sabi appears in the hut's dry rock walls and wind-scoured isolation.

The aesthetic conveyed by these terms opens up a distinctive angle on natural beauty for hikers, especially in the United States. So much of our focus is on the "grand," whether canyons or tetons. Colonists construed grand nature as something transcending history and substituting for the local history they did not have. It was even deployed to nationalistic ends when Thomas Jefferson went to Europe and, awed by the civilization there but not wanting to be outdone, lifted up the vast nature of the United States as a source of pride and distinction worthy of recognition by Europeans who might otherwise look down on the upstart county and its uncouth inhabitants.

Attuned to the beauty that Japanese highlight with such terms as *wabi* and *sabi*, we can shift our focus from large-scale—bigger is better?—objects in nature to smaller things, like the smooth pebble I found yesterday beside the Dry River, with a band of quartz running through its equator, or the stick I picked up with a labyrinth of grooves bored into its surface by a long-gone beetle.

Appreciation of the beauty of nature in these and other ways can affect us ethically. Simon James notes that

> the aesthetic sensitivity to the world engendered by the practice of, say, flower arranging translates into a particular aesthetic appreciation of the world. Seeing the delicate beauty of flower arrangements, the artist comes to see the beauty inherent in all things—like a *haiku* poet, perhaps. And just as a sense of this beauty causes him to treat the flowers, twigs, and pebbles with which he works with respect, so he gradually becomes gentler in his dealings with all things. His aesthetic appreciation has naturally engendered a particular ethical comportment.[110]

Or, as I once said in a debate with a colleague eager to sacrifice religion and feeling on the altar of rationality, "For every person who becomes an environmentalist after crunching numbers about ecological degradation, there are ten who become environmentalists after a powerful experience of beauty out in nature."

In addition to the arts that James mentions, on the trail I've found myself thinking about tea ceremony. Jakuan Sōtaku, who in 1828 composed the *Zen Tea Record* (*Zencharoku*), used the expression *cha-zen ichimi*, "tea and Zen—one taste." Echoing the Zen admonition to give oneself fully to the action at hand, he tells his readers that when doing an action in the tea ceremony "immerse your heart and mind fully in it alone and give no thought whatever to other matters."[111] Maybe hiking is one taste with Zen and tea ceremony: like in meditation and the ceremony, when hiking one slows things down, becomes more aware of the breath, perseveres in pain, and stays in the moment while going forward, one breath and one step at a time. This practice of concentration and immersion gets complemented by four values said to permeate the tea ceremony: *kei*, respect; *wa*, harmony; *sei*, purity; and *jaku*, tranquility. All four apply to hiking as well.

Respect extends beyond our attitude toward others. On the trail it can take the form of reverence: the impulse to bow at the sunset, stand in awe over the fern frond jutting up from under rotting leaves, and appreciate the dignity of a solitary white pine. Such reverential wonder is a doorway to understanding in one's gut—not just in one's head—that the plants and critters are miraculous living systems, play an ecological role that humans are only beginning to comprehend, and deserve our respect. Maybe this is what animists feel when they walk through forests. Maybe this is what the day-hikers with the sodas are *not* feeling: the smoker extinguishes his cigarette on the trail while his girlfriend tromps across fragile alpine heather to seat herself on a rock.

Perhaps it was such reverence that Aldo Leopold felt when he saw the light disappear from the eyes of a dying wolf, or that led him to declare, "A thing is right when it tends to preserve the integrity, stability, and beauty of the biotic community. It is wrong when it tends otherwise."[112] When we comprehend the rightness of a thing in this sense, we may come to value it and protect it, or at least complain about the bulldozers that harm it.

At the practical level, when I feel appreciation and respect for things around me, whether wild blueberries, an old shirt, or pieces of firewood, I feel drawn to use them respectfully, without carelessness or waste. This has been a core value of the original inhabitants of this place, Turtle Island, who have shown respect to the animals they've hunted, thanked them for offering up their bodies, and used as much of the animals as possible. In this way they exhibit what Gary Snyder has termed "good manners."

The Japanese have an expression for not wasting: *mono no shō o tsukusu*, "to use completely the nature of things." Get the most out of each thing. Use it as long—and in as many ways—as possible. Burn firewood completely and, if at home, spread the ashes on the vegetable garden. As the shirt loses buttons, sew on new ones. Patch the elbows. Stitch frayed hems back into place. And when the collar splits and the cuffs open into tassels, use the shirt as a rag. Many of us already practice this version of frugality when we compost and recycle.

In this spirit, limit the things you acquire. Don't buy that new winter parka. Combine the one you already have with that down vest in the back of the closet. Preserve old friends—the pants you wore to Benares, the fleece you dug out of the pack on the top of Mount Whitney, the patched Gore-Tex shell that kept you from getting soaked in the Hoh rainforest on the way up to the Blue Glacier at the base of Mount Olympus. And should your body dictate wisely that you need to get a smaller, lighter pack as your back starts to break down in your fifties, give the old external-frame Kelty or the Mountainsmith behemoth to an organization like the Appalachian Mountain Club that tries to get young people out into the woods. As Thoreau said, "Simplify, simplify, simplify"; Buddhists might say, "Give, give, give."

When we mend, reuse, cherish, and share possessions, they take on more meaning, more value—and maybe even a bit of wabi-sabi!—as they age with us. This is how we honor them on their own pilgrimages through this world.

This ethic may seem self-evident on an extended backpacking trip when we mend the split crotch in our rain pants and find multiple uses for socks, but back home, in the midst of material bounty, it may seem trivial. Why do I have to think about other uses for this stained T-shirt when new one costs less than ten bucks? Can't I just throw away this black sock with a hole in the heel? Do I really have to go out of my way to compost a random piece of paper towel rather than drop it in the trashcan? When we're hurrying or our schedules are packed tight, our ego tells us that treating things with respect takes too much time, especially given the dollar figure we might put on those minutes relative to what we think our time is worth.

But to express respect is to move through nature—and life—with grace, like the gentle demeanor of the host of a tea ceremony. To move gracefully is to move lightly, disturbing little, leaving no trace, or at least as small a trace as you can.

Being reverent slides over into being humble in the face of the power of the wild. Survival of the fittest is no abstraction when fording a tributary of the Elwa after a downpour in the Olympics or an avalanche crashes down in your direction as you negotiate a technical pitch on the way to Camp Three on Pumori. Nature can bite you, maybe even devour you. Lizzie Bourne learned this the hard way here in the White Mountains back in 1855.[113]

The second tea value is *wa*, harmony. It refers to matching bowls with the season and to the flowing ease with which the host performs the tea ritual. To be in harmony is to be attuned to what is happening around us. A skilled hiker picks up on subtle shifts in the breeze and clouds. She pays attention, not talking incessantly or getting lost in a train wreck of thoughts. To be in harmony is to be in the woods on nature's terms, not on terms dictated by our ego.

Purity, *sei*, refers to purification done by the guest while waiting to enter the teahouse, the simplicity and cleanliness of the space itself, and the way the ceremony clears one's mind of worldly concerns. Reflecting on a scroll (*kakemono*) in a teahouse alcove (*tokonoma*), D. T. Suzuki once wrote, "By seeing the kakemono in the tokonoma and the flower in the vase, one's sense of smell is cleansed; by listening to the boiling of water in the iron kettle and to the dripping of water from the bamboo pipe, one's ears are cleansed; by tasting tea one's mouth is cleansed; and by handling the tea utensils one's sense of touch is cleansed. When thus all the sense organs are cleansed, the mind itself is cleansed of defilements."[114]

In traditional Buddhism, the main defilements are greed, ill will, and ignorance—the "three poisons." Buddhists also talk about the five hindrances: desire, anger, sloth, agitation, and doubt. Though there are direct antidotes to these "unwholesome" mental states—in the case of the three poisons, giving to cultivate generosity, extending love to cultivate loving-kindness, and meditating to cultivate wisdom—much of the Buddhist response to them has to do with restraint, so much so that some have characterized Buddhism as offering an ethic of restraint. We see this especially in the five moral precepts: to *refrain* from harming, from taking what has not been given, from lying, from engaging in sexual misconduct, and from using intoxicants.

This brings us to the fourth tea value, *jaku*, tranquility. Standing on the ridge, my mind is still as I take in the view of the Presidentials laid out before me. I'm tired but calm.

But my mind is not completely still, for I find myself thinking about how these core values of tea and the Zen aesthetic described by Hisamatsu go beyond beauty and refinement and encompass the mental states that are present when we're moved by beauty on the trail. Maybe our minds need to be still, tranquil, open, receptive, and respectful for us to pay sustained attention to things, see them clearly, and by extension, appreciate their beauty. Maybe these mental states are the foundation of powerful experiences of beauty and, as such, constitute a bridge between spirituality and aesthetics. As we saw in Suzuki's statement about tea ceremony, this marriage of spirit and beauty also slides into the realm of ethics, where the cleansing, stillness, and vision take on moral significance—whether cleansing us of mental defilements like greed and ill will or leading us to value and care for the things that we now appreciate in their suchness and beauty.

Resting here on Crawford Path, I think about this question of ethics in relation to hiking. I start imagining how hiking might relate to something I explored with my students last semester, the six *pāramitās* or perfections of Mahāyāna Buddhism: perfected generosity, moral discipline, patience, vigorous exertion, meditative concentration, and wisdom. These virtues are cultivated by the bodhisattva, the accomplished being who postpones her own complete liberation from the cycle of rebirth to stick around to help others, or as one metaphor expresses it, to lead others up the mountain. To equip herself for this compassionate intervention, the bodhisattva works over many lifetimes to perfect herself.

In the case of a bodhisattva, "perfected" generosity refers to the open, giving spirit of a person always willing to "be there" for others in concrete, helpful ways. For the laity in Asian Buddhism, generosity gets cultivated through such core practices as giving alms to monks on their begging rounds or donating to temples. In addition to generating merit, the act of giving provides an opportunity to let go, to practice nonattachment. In this way, although the giving may leave the layperson with a net loss at the material level, spiritually she is better off. This angle on generosity accords with the proverb, "The generous man enriches himself by giving; the miser hoards himself poor."

Hikers know this to be true. When pausing for a break, the bag of trail mix gets passed around. Extra layers are offered to the chilly hiker as the sun goes down. We share a tent. My mac and cheese is your mac and cheese, and everyone gets a bite out of the apple. We are a collection of bodies chugging along the trail together, sweating together (or shivering together), getting sore together, sitting around the fire together, jumping into the brook together, tucking into the tent together.

As they pass around a cigarette and the last ounces of the Diet Coke, the day-hikers, too, are familiar with how people can bond through acts of generosity. Dragging off the same Marlboro and swigging out of the same bottle promotes the communitas seen in the pilgrims to

Mecca or devotees of Mary in the candlelight procession at Lourdes. No wonder colleges have gone beyond tugs of war and barbecues on the quad and incorporated hiking and backpacking into their efforts to build community during first-year orientation.

The second perfection, of moral discipline, refers in part to following the Buddhist precepts, whether the five observed by the laity, the ten practiced by a novice, or the 200-plus in the code that guides the lives of fully ordained monks and nuns. In the woods, my monastic code is the seven principles of "leave no trace":

1. Plan ahead and prepare.

2. Travel and camp on durable surfaces.

3. Dispose of waste properly.

4. Leave what you find.

5. Minimize campfire impacts.

6. Respect wildlife.

7. Be considerate of other visitors.

To this standard list I add an eighth: pay attention.

Perfected patience is the willingness to keep engaging in meditative practice and helping others for long years without getting frustrated with an apparent lack of progress. This attribute is similar to the quiet strength of committed hikers, who persevere on long days with aching shoulders and sore feet, tolerating the pain while enjoying the hike.

The perfection of exertion refers to a Buddhist's devotion to the path, to the vigor she expresses each morning as she gets up to sit in meditation, chant, and help others. The backpacker rises early, too, and cooks breakfast, packs up, and heads back onto the trail.

As far as the fifth and sixth perfections are concerned, the perfection of meditative concentration is perhaps most akin to the "zone" hikers find themselves in on the trail. Perfected wisdom is insight into the impermanence and emptiness of all things, a discernment of how people cling and suffer, and an attentiveness that sees things as they are, in their suchness. In the Whites today, granite, lichen, stunted spruce, wind, and cloud present themselves on Mount Pierce.

In Zen, these Mahāyāna virtues are colored by Daoist notions of virtue, or *de*, a character that appears in the title of the classic *Daodejing*. The English word *virtue* derives from *virtus*, "innate power," as indicated by the related term *virility*. Similarly, *de* is the potency that makes it possible for animals to do their particular thing: the innate ability of a hawk to fly, a frog to catch bugs with its tongue, a human to reason and deploy an opposable thumb. This power appears all around us—in the making of a web, the blossoming of a rose, the strange ability of a baby to hold on to your finger more firmly that you'd expect. The ability of a person to walk upright along the Dry River and then climb up to a perch looking out at the Presidentials.

Chinese also construe *de* as a knack. The Daoist sage Zhuangzi detected de in the ability of the butcher who can cut up an ox without hitting bones and has never had to sharpen his knife. When we get in touch with this power, we can act more intuitively and spontaneously ("naturally"), without forcing things. This way of acting is *wu-wei*, literally "nonaction," but better translated as "unforced action," or "effortless action." We see it in our ability to breathe, perform actions we've mastered, and step on flat places along the trail without thinking consciously about where to place our feet.

Daoism also champions the sage who has rejected conventions and the discriminating intellect that accompanies them. Having recovered his original naturalness—the "uncarved block"[115]—this person comes across as dull and ignorant. He lives a life of simplicity, has few desires, and moves through life like water: yielding, not contending—the true hiker. And like many hikers, the Daoist sage is said to prefer dwelling in the mountains. A Chinese character for "sagely hermit" or "immortal" is *shen* (仙), composed of the character for "person" (人) and the character for "mountain" (山). A true mountain person is attuned to how the Dao moves in and around himself.

Maybe it all comes down to Gary Snyder's "etiquette of freedom," which applies equally to Zen practitioners and hikers: "Practically speaking, a life that is vowed to simplicity, appropriate boldness, good humor, gratitude, unstinting work and play, and lots of walking brings us close to the actually existing world and its wholeness. . . . No expectations, alert and sufficient, grateful and careful, generous and direct. A calm and clarity attend us in the moment we are wiping grease off our hands and glancing up at the passing clouds."[116] And, Snyder has added, this ethic also consists of knowing one's place, one's bioregion, with all of its natural and human history.

To this end I sometimes bring guides to local wildflowers and birds, and try to memorize the names that accompany the photos of familiar plants. But I wonder: is this conscientious, studious mind that craves knowledge the type of consciousness I want to foster when out on the trail? Maybe I should burn the field guides and try *not* to learn the names of flowers and trees, try not to diminish my ability to see them just as they are. The Bible tells us, "Out of the ground the Lord God formed every animal of the field and every bird of the air, and brought them to the man to see what he would call them; and whatever the man called every living creature, that was its name" (Genesis 2:19), which makes me wonder whether Adam and Eve's loss of innocence and expulsion from the Garden of Eden had more to do with naming things than with biting into forbidden fruit. Perhaps our task is to let go of the discriminating, categorizing mind that tries to identify flowers and, instead, to see them more clearly and vividly in their suchness, as they present themselves free of the names attached to them by Adam in the beginning of time or Carl Linnaeus in the eighteenth century.

That being said, to learn the names of flora and fauna and get a handle on their ecological niches is to understand the processes linking the "ten-thousand things" in my region and gain a better sense of the changes that are happening to the ecosystems in which I reside. I do need to know the White Mountains better. Through knowing them I can appreciate them if not love them, which does seem to be the first step to actually working to protect them. Maybe the koan here is the koan at the heart of Zen: how to be able to think about things *and* empty ourselves of thought, how to discriminate, analyze, and understand what we experience while also being able to let go of that cognition and be filled by what we experience with no sense of separation.

As I take another swig from my bottle and start getting ready to descend to Crawford Notch, my groggy brain grapples with this dilemma and then, in but a few moments, as if with a tired sigh, lets it go. Too much to ponder in the middle of the day's exertion.

NINE

Return

帰

KI —
"RETURN"

It grants freedom, expansion, and release. Untied. Unstuck. Crazy
for a while. It breaks taboo, it verges on transgression, it teaches
humility. Going out—fasting—singing alone—talking across the
species boundaries—praying—giving thanks—coming back.

—GARY SNYDER[117]

We shall not cease from exploration
And the end of all of our exploring
Will be to arrive where we started
And know the place for the first time.

—T. S. ELIOT, "LITTLE GIDDING"[118]

As I HIT THE FIRST STEEP SECTION on the descent to Crawford
Notch, my right knee starts talking to me. I can almost hear
the crackling in the cartilage-free zone beneath my patella. As I side-
step my way down, I start thinking about geological time, and feel
grateful for the winds and rain that have brought the Appalachians
down from over 40,000 feet to a size my knees can manage in an
overnight hike with minimal gear. To distract myself further from
the jabbing sensation at the end of my right femur, I start imagining
dinner at the Chinese restaurant in Lincoln. And the peanut M&Ms
for sale in the minimart by the Route 93 on-ramp. I also start thank-
ing my trekking poles for taking some of the stress off my knees.

The trail is busy today, and every few minutes I stand aside to
let people climb up past me: an AMC-organized hike with a young

guide in the lead, hut workers with boxes stacked on wooden pack frames, parents with reluctant kids, kids with reluctant parents. Several times I get passed from behind. One guy, about my age, glides down from rock to rock like a teenager. I wonder how he does it. He must have more cartilage behind his kneecaps than I do. I also daydream about how hard it was for Ethan Crawford to make this trail and wonder whether he could have imagined that the path he built would still be used—and by herds of people—two hundred years later.

After I emerge back out on Route 302, I pause before crossing. Cars and motorcycles zoom by at what feels like maniacal speeds. A wave of fear flows through my chest as I wait for a gap. After a minute I cross the road and head up and over an embankment to the parking lot of the AMC Highland Center. At the south end of the lot I see the hiker who bounded past me back on the trail and ask him and his friend whether they can give me a lift to my car, five miles down the road at the Dry River trailhead.

An hour later I'm sitting with a cold Heineken and a thousand calories of sauce-covered splendor at Chieng Gardens in Lincoln. My indulging reveals to the young couple at the next table that while pilgrimage may be painful, it isn't completely austere. It can get playful if not raucous. This ludic component usually happens at the end of the journey, when pilgrims give up their asceticism and celebrate. In many pilgrimage traditions it is as if Fat Tuesday were shifted to the day after Easter Monday, following rather than anticipating Lent. Japanese call it *shōjin otoshi*, the dropping of abstinence, which traditionally took place in lodgings—stocked with sake and female entertainers—that lined the streets of gateway villages at the base of sacred mountains. On the last day of the hajj, Muslim pilgrims feast. On Easter Sunday, Christians feast, freeing themselves from the austerity of their journey across the forty days leading up to it.

By the time I get to Boston, I'm hungry again, so I stop at a Shaw's market. Though toughened by the trip and probably striking other shoppers as feral, I find the store intimidating. I feel rattled at the sight of jug upon jug of milk in the dairy section, an entire aisle of breakfast cereals, and enough potato chips for a hundred Super Bowl parties. Jumpy after driving two hours in traffic on Route 93, my nerves struggle with the fluorescent light. I cut my shopping short, resting content with a dozen eggs, three apples, one dark chocolate bar, and a chunk of cheddar. Now I just want to get back to our condo and shut the door behind me.

Across religions, the last act of pilgrimage is heading home and resuming one's ordinary life, what Victor Turner termed "reaggregation" into the social structure. Perhaps not permanently, but the arc is one of return. This motif extends beyond pilgrimage in the formal sense. At the end of their exodus, the Israelites come out of the desert, out of exile, and return to their homeland. Muhammad hikes down off Mount Hira and back into Mecca with his first revelation from Allah. Buddha gets up from under the bodhi tree and rejoins his fellow seekers in the Deer Park near Benares. Odysseus reaches Penelope after a harrowing (and hallowing?) journey home. In the Ten Oxherding Pictures, the Zen seeker ventures out, finds the ox (wakes up!), and then, with awakening fully embodied, returns to the "marketplace," back to his town, the world of relationships, commerce, politics. But not as the same person. Now he is reaching out to his neighbors with "bliss-bestowing hands."

At the end of a pilgrimage, with blisters and stronger legs, with stories, amulets, vials of holy water, and maybe even a new name or title, the pilgrim puts her feet up. Likewise, the hiker pilgrim plops down on the couch, transformed by the journey, often in ways that become evident only after reengaging with the people from whom she had parted. She may find that she's viewing her home and workplace in a different light. She may not feel comfortable back in the roles and routines she had left behind. As I often say to students who are about to study overseas, "In some ways the real learning begins after you get back. That's when you notice how you've changed. You may find that your friends are still on the same old wavelength and you're now on a different one. Or you may find yourself seeing your country from a new angle. Culture shock is educational, but reverse culture shock is often much more intense and illuminating." This holds for backpacking as well.

Sometimes I further warn my students, "Friends and loved ones may not want to hear your stories about the encounters you had, the travails you endured. They may not want to see your photos of the Ganges, the Great Wall, and Ryōanji, or at least no more than the first five shots. If you're coming back from East Asia, they may make clumsy jokes about whether you'll ever be able to use a fork again or, appallingly, comment on how 'months of eating rice with chopsticks didn't make your eyes go slanty.'" Soon after I returned to the U.S. from my initial five years in Japan, I actually found myself on the receiving end of that comment, which made me feel all the more like Rip Van Winkle.

Unless they die on the trail, hikers, too, return with images and memories. Not that we remember our time on the trail with photographic clarity. We may succumb to selective memory or selective forgetting. Hikers back off the trail may remember the view of Mount Washington from six miles away while forgetting the diarrhea. Or the other way around: going on and on about loose bowels, rain, and the bugs but forgetting the peak's majesty and the joy of squealing under a frigid waterfall on the south side of the mountain.

Being out on the trail can transform us, usually in ways that become evident only upon our return. It can bestow blessings on us. It can teach us lessons. Maybe nothing earthshaking, but at least a few learnings and unlearnings that color how we live back at home.

For example, like most returned pilgrims, I find that off the trail I take fewer things for granted. Hot showers *are* a miracle, as are flush toilets. Owning a refrigerator, and having beer in it, feels luxurious, as does the potable water that flows from the faucet.

But the condo feels cluttered. Tchotchkes on the shelves, an army of shirts in the closet, all sorts of pots and pans. I start asking myself, "Do we really need all of these dishes? Why do we have three salad bowls?" (I'm less willing to ask such questions about my books and outdoor gear—my main objects of attachment.) Somehow a part of my psyche is perpetually drawn to the simplicity of carrying my home on my back: a tent as the house, a stuff sack as the refrigerator and cupboard, another sack as my dresser and closet, and a small pouch as my bathroom cabinet. My sense of "enough" has shifted.

With part of my psyche still out on the trail, activity around me feels frenetic. A guy in a three-piece suit jogs to the bus stop in Watertown Square. Other drivers seem worked into a frenzy as they cut me off on Galen Street. At the YMCA, men in the locker room hurry to put their clothes on, as if they're running late for a meeting. On any given Saturday parents scurry from rink to gym to mall as they juggle their kids' games and their own vague desires to buy things. It makes me want to retreat to a campfire several miles from the nearest automobile, or at least open up space in my calendar to help me to avoid this freneticism and "live deliberately."

Whenever I return from a backpacking trip, some things even strike me as surreal: people in a trance as they push overflowing carts at the supermarket, families lined up in front of televisions for hours on end, kids texting in their laps at the dinner table, actors in commercials pretending they're real people with incontinence or erectile dysfunction.

In the middle of all of this I often feel detached, at least for the first few days. I feel like an anthropologist in my own village, observing all the odd behaviors. As things swirl around me, I also savor traces of the tranquility that I bring back from the trail. I find myself less reactive and more accepting.

Thanks to sustained exertion on the trail—keeping my legs moving even when my quads are groaning or the pack is cutting into my right trapezius—my perseverance and stamina get enhanced: I corral my hunger until it's time for dinner; I hang in there with tasks I really don't want to do; I take deep breaths and resign myself to being stuck in traffic. But this doesn't feel like an enhancement of willpower: rather than gritting my teeth and exerting myself as an act of will, I act out of calmness, out of supple spaciousness rather than tight constriction. For hikers as well as pilgrims, "The art is to learn to master today's unavoidable situation with as much equanimity as we can muster, in preparation for facing its sequel tomorrow."[119]

With the calm strength cultivated by backpacking, I tend to slow things down and savor the moment more. I am more apt to "take my time" (a strange expression) cooking meals. I rush less when mowing the lawn, weeding the garden, and raking dunes of leaves in the fall. I appreciate my body's ability to do these physical acts on our little piece of land. I sometimes feel joy as I do them, more as a meditative practice than a "chore." In winter I get my pant legs wet and my mind refreshed as I walk through ten inches of snow to pour coffee grounds, eggshells, and banana peels onto the compost pile, remembering how my gaiters have kept dew from soaking my pant legs when I've hiked through grassy stretches at dawn.

As the Zen adage would have it, I chop wood and carry water. Small tasks, daily chances to give myself away—chop, carry, rake, shovel, vacuum, wash. In Kyoto today the monks are doing their samu: wiping wood verandas with rags, weeding rows of cabbage, chopping carrots for gruel. At home I do my samu, and my labors are colored by not only Zen monastic life but the tasks I've done at campsites over six decades.

The calm spaciousness fostered on the trail helps me recover the pleasure of doing tasks thoroughly, without leaving them half done or the space half messy. When I stop juggling multiple tasks and objects, I'm more apt to practice what I preach and pour myself into one activity at a time. I can better focus on the action at hand, mindfully, carefully, and perhaps beautifully. The Japanese have an expression, *kichinto suru*, which can be translated as "do something properly, in the way it ought to be done." Combined with a long tradition of craftsmanship, this commitment to doing things in the right manner may account for some of the refinement and grace in Japanese living. Do the task as a creative expression, then clean up and put away the tools, just like when a backpacker scatters rocks used in a fire circle and packs up her gear. No clutter, no mess, no loose ends. Leave no trace.

Back off the trail, I also find myself wanting to take care of my body, which today is still sore, nicked, and grizzly from scampering up the Dry River Valley. Last night, at the end of my first full day back from the Whites, I stretched before plunking down on the couch. This morning, from a place other than "ought," I headed over to the YMCA and, to open up muscle kinks from the hike, swam some leisurely laps—what I call "water yoga"—then sat in the hot tub. As I leaned back into the jets, my imagination took me back several decades to the Northwest and diving under waves as they crashed against sandbars on the Olympic Peninsula, jumping into pools beside boulders on the Quinault, and sweating with friends in the Kennedy Hot Springs.

Following a hike, I'm usually quieter. I listen more and talk less. This may be the most important boon. For many of us caught up in a high-tech, high-speed, high-stress lifestyle, the biggest challenge is knowing how to slow our mouths down, how to be attentive to others, perhaps even be a strong, silent type. Hiking, like physical labor and monastic life, can also help us clean up the content of our speaking. The "right speech" part of the Eightfold Path directs us to refrain not only from lying but from divisive speech, harsh speech, and idle gossip, and extended time on the trail helps me practice this.

Though probably not a hiker or a Buddhist, a fellow I met a few years back on Vinalhaven seemed to embody this. He is the owner of a boat that is equipped with a crane strong enough to lift blocks of granite for bulkheads there on the island. I met him at an art gallery, at an opening that he, like me, might not have wanted to attend. Before I walked over and introduced myself, he stood glancing at vacationers, several of whom were making comments about the paintings on display. He seemed to be tracking what they were saying, and he exuded a kind of knowing that I couldn't quite fathom. Silent waters do run deep, or as the Japanese prefer to phrase it, "skilled hawks conceal their claws."

At one point he started talking with another islander about a sick neighbor. Their smudged jeans and scarred boots spoke of labor. Their creased faces told stories of erosion—waves cutting into the beach on the east side of the island, ice working the seams in the abandoned quarries, and winds carving down from the White Mountains and into their foreheads. They both had stubby fingers, callused, I assumed, from changing oil, hauling lobster pots, and scraping barnacles. They both exemplified the notion that for many people a day of no work is, in fact, a day of no eating.

These two men also got me thinking about the congruence between rural life in New England, Zen monasticism, and backpacking. Or more precisely, bored with the art opening, I found myself filled with images from those three domains, images that seem to fit together or at least complement each other like in a mosaic: cutting brush, sweeping temple verandas, gathering firewood; repairing fishing nets, serving tea, pitching a tent; hooking the rope below lobster buoys and winding it around the winch, raking gravel in a rock garden, stuffing a sleeping bag into a sack; drinking coffee from chipped mugs in the sugar shack, slurping miso soup out of a bowl, gobbling ramen out of the pot next to the campfire. Wool sweater, canvas cargo pants, and boots; a monk's blue *samu-e* work clothes and straw sandals; polypro, fleece, and hiking boots. Working and walking in one's body with aches, calluses, and cuts. Nothing flashy here. Low-tech, low-hype, low-ego.

As I do chores, my body reminds me of things I've noticed on New England trails: dusty hands, dry hemlock bark; wrinkled face, burls on maples; scuffed boots, exposed roots; freckles on cheeks, lichen on glacial erratics. Like the limbs of hemlocks creaking in the wind above the tent site by the Dry River, my knees crackled as I picked lettuce this morning.

Living and hiking in New England even colors my meditation. As I settle on the front edge of the cushion up in the attic zendō and fold my knees, stiff from the descent along Crawford Path, I think of the rock I sat on the other day beside the Dry River. With a straight back I sit on the cushions, taking as my role model the granite peaks up in New Hampshire: silent, immovable, strong. I sit weathered, like Mount Pierce. My joints ache and my face is dry, like creaking hemlocks along the Amanoosuc River. What I'm practicing is not some sort of generic or universal Zen but a form that has been colored by my walking and living in this region.

Simply put, one fruit of my hiking is the grounding of me—and my spiritual practice—fully in this place. The boundaries between my body, my spiritual path, and the rugged nature in New England are blurry.

For many of us, hiking is an excellent way to deepen our connection to nature in and around us. When in the backcountry, we have to pay attention to our surroundings. We have to keep a close eye on what is at our feet, looking out for rocks or roots that can sprain an ankle. Depending on the route, we may need to track landmarks and trail junctions in sync with a topo map, or if off trail, our compass bearing. We need to be vigilant for poison ivy, and keep an eye out for animals, whether camp robbers swooping down after gorp or bears catching a whiff of our dinner. We monitor our water supply and know when we'll next be able to fill our water bottles. We track the weather, staying aware of the clouds and shifts in temperature. Then there's nature in our bodies: Am I hydrated enough? Am I consuming enough calories to keep my muscles going? Is the skin on my face getting burned by the sun? Any hot spots on my feet? Any insistent pains in my legs? Any giardia starting to reproduce in my lower GI?

Hiking motivates me to cultivate this connection to nature at home. I track what weather is coming our way from New York State. I monitor harbingers of seasonal shifts, whether the first crocuses of spring or Canada geese flying south in grand Vs in October (at least they used to). I notice raspberry shoots invading the far edge of the garden, listen to squirrels jumping onto the roof from the maple tree by the driveway, and watch cardinals build a nest, hatch eggs, and teach fledglings to fly from the Japanese maple off the back deck. I watch a red-tailed hawk, perched in the beech snag out behind our neighbor's house, scanning for movement in the knotweed beyond our garden. I go for walks along the Charles to look for fish and cormorants. As Snyder reminds us, the wild is right here. Ants file into the kitchen looking for water. Dandelions push up through cracks in the sidewalk down on Pearl Street.

At the very least, time on the trail, and outside on pilgrimages, enhances our motivation to avoid doing what so many of us do: cut ourselves off from nature by retreating into our climate-controlled spaces and digital lives.

In the days following a pilgrimage to the mountains, I feel something else I've brought back from the trail: the recognition that I am animal. Though walking in the wilderness near bears and cougars may remind us of this, we don't have to be twenty miles into the backcountry. Even back home I remember that I'm a critter living in nature. I am nesting in this condo. I eat, sweat, and grow hair. I feel the urge to reproduce. I forage for food in the kitchen. I burrow down under the covers to sleep. A shot of adrenaline surges into my muscles when I hear something go bump in the night.

This deepening of our felt connection to nature *as* nature can in turn deepen our commitment to the nature—the worked over and polluted nature—that is close as hand. As Gary Snyder puts it, the purpose of wilderness exploration is "to be able to come back to the lowlands and see all the land about us, agricultural, suburban, urban, as part of the same territory—never totally ruined, never completely unnatural. It can be restored, and humans could live in considerable numbers on much of it. Great Brown Bear is walking with us, Salmon swimming upstream with us, as we stroll a city street."[120]

With this awareness, we can avoid getting attached to the backcountry when planning hikes. We can avoid the pitfall of fetishizing wilderness and putting all of our efforts into protecting "untouched" or "pristine" places (not that they still exist). Indeed, many of us direct our focus to remote mountains at the exclusion of nearby hills, woods, city parks, and our own backyard. As Michael Pollan points out,

> "All or nothing," says the wilderness ethic, and in fact we've ended up with a landscape in America that conforms to that injunction remarkably well. Thanks to exactly this kind of either/or thinking, Americans have done an admirable job of drawing lines around certain sacred areas (we did invent the wilderness idea) and a terrible job of managing the rest of our land. The reason is not hard to find: the only environmental ethic we have has nothing useful to say about those areas outside the line. Once a landscape is no longer "virgin" it is typically written off as fallen, lost to nature, irredeemable. We hand it over to

the jurisdiction of that other sacrosanct American ethic: laissez-fair economics.[121]

Perhaps the benefit we should seek in our pilgrimages into nature is not a direct experience of the most "awesome" peak or the most "virgin" wilderness but the ability to pay close attention to the nature that is happening all around us—the ants filing into the kitchen, the dandelions pushing up through the grass, the pigeons foraging in the park. The vision we need to expand is not across the Wrangell–St. Elias range in Alaska but toward the squirrel that just crawled up onto the back deck.

The smaller-scale nature and wildness close to home offer the added bonus of being accessible not only to younger, ultra-fit hikers but to older, sluggish walkers, and perhaps even to those with walkers, or those who move around on chairs with wheels.

So how might we go on a pilgrimage to Boston Common or our own back yard? Was not that cumulonimbus cloud above Beacon Street more magnificent than Everest as it rose with misty cliffs, dark gorges, and a lofty summit to an elevation of well over 35,000 feet? If only we can see it. The Himalayas may seem permanent— and indeed they are denser and more enduring than an August thunderhead over Brookline—but from the long-range vision of a geologist, or in the eyes of Dōgen, they are "constantly walking." Make no mistake—they too are temporary configurations of energy, passing waves on the great ocean of the universe. It's just that mountains are rising up and breaking more slowly than that six-foot wave that shot me along its face last summer off Nauset Light.

When all is said and done, perhaps the most advanced wilderness savvy, the true bragging rights, belong not to the climber who bags five peaks in one day on a Teton traverse or to Reinhold Messner for his solo ascents with no bottled oxygen, but to pilgrims who can see all of nature in a pigeon pecking for crumbs in Cambridge.

To facilitate this seeing, Gary Snyder urges us to know our biore-gion, even if we occasionally wander far afield on our hikes and pilgrimages. After the journey is over and we've shared at least a few stories, we rebuild our home as our base camp, our sanctuary. We reinhabit and restore the place of that home, even if a crowded neighborhood in Queens. Snyder urges us

> to see our country in terms of its landforms, plant life, weather patterns, and season changes—its whole natural history before the net of political jurisdiction was cast over it. People are challenged to become "reinhabitory"— that is, to become people who are learning to live and think "as if" they were totally engaged with their place for the long future. This doesn't mean the return to a primitive lifestyle or utopian provincialism; it simply implies an engagement with community and a search for the sustain-able sophisticated mix of economic practices that would enable people to live regionally and yet learn from and contribute to a planetary society.[122]

In doing this you take the long view and live "as though your grand-children would also be alive, in this land, carrying on the work we're doing right now, with deepening insight."[123] From our grounding in a place, we can, like the returned pilgrim, venture back out into the world and perhaps even take steps to protect it, whether the nearby Charles River or the desert wilderness of southern Utah.

The first step to being fully in one's home place is to study it. What is the bedrock, and how old is it? What was this place like during the ice age? Who lived here before the Puritans arrived? What did the indigenous people call this place before settlers dispossessed them? What plants and animals inhabit my block?[124] Where does my water come from? Where does my sewage go? Which birds summer in and around my quarter acre? Which birds live here year-round? How can I clean up my neighborhood? How can I get involved in preserving the less-tarnished spots in my area? Not that this is easy—all too often, even after coming back from extended time on the trail, we can fall back into our air-conditioned bubbles, driving everywhere, walking on flat sidewalks, ignoring the weather, hurrying to appointments, and burying ourselves in our devices, oblivious of the trees, birds, and myriad other beings up and down the street.

We've all been asked the question "Where do you live?" Most of us answer by naming a town or a part of town. If we live in a city, we might refer to landmarks like freeway exits, major intersections, or prominent buildings—human artifacts. How might we answer that question in relation to nature? What is your bioregion? In what watershed do you reside? What are the natural features around your abode in the four cardinal directions? What plants and animals live their lives alongside you? What "weeds" are outside expressing their own desire to flourish as fellow living beings? What bugs live in the soil? What critters regularly pass through your neighborhood? How does water move through it? Wendy Johnson urges us "to become intimate with the wildness and deep rhythms of the place where you live, and to listen to the particular, distinct voice of your watershed."[125] It does not need to be the entire watershed. Maybe just the area we can walk through in a day of wandering. Thoreau thought about this, and he claimed that the area we can get to know intimately over the course of a lifetime is twenty square miles.[126]

My home is the second floor and attic of a house in Watertown, Massachusetts, three miles west of where a hardwood forest was leveled four hundred years ago to construct Harvard Square and six miles as the seagull flies from the Atlantic Ocean. I live in the watershed of the Charles River, a third of a mile north of where it flows over a dam for a mill that has long disappeared. Our condo is on the south flank of Palfrey Hill, one side of which is seven acres of oaks, maples, and beeches. Just east of us is a valley, with a few tennis courts and sports fields for Watertown High School. Wind often surges through it from the west, chilling us in winter when we walk around the track or stand there at night to look for falling stars.

From the window of the attic zendō I look south across rooftops, eye to eye with the steeple of Philips Congregational Church and, farther away, the gothic tower at the center of Perkins School for the Blind. During colder months I watch parallel columns of smoke and steam rise from chimneys. Across the valley, oak, maple, hemlock, and spruce provide infrastructure for gray squirrels, robins, and wasps (the bee kind). They sink roots down through urban detritus into duff, scat, bones, and gravel that have been weathered into soil since the last glacier receded twelve thousand years ago. Their roots pull water that has fallen from clouds drifting up along the Appalachians from the Gulf of Mexico or riding the jet stream across the continent from the Pacific. Surviving in their exurban, post-industrial nook, these trees express themselves as naturally as any redwood in Humboldt County, though with more initials carved in their trunks and more heavy metal in their limbs.

This is my place in nature. Granted, it's a spot that has been infused with chemicals from crumbling factories and smoked by traffic stalled on the Mass Pike a mile away on the other side of the Charles. But nature is happening all around me. In my watershed, the murky river bends itself for eighty miles across eastern Massachusetts from tributary rills in Hopkinton, getting fed along the way by six dozen streams. Canada geese and mallards congregate downstream from where Boston Scientific renovated Aetna Mills. Chased by the occasional striper, alewife dart up to the waterfall at the dam. Here on our street a gang of crows squawk in the huge oak that leans ominously over cars parked two houses away. A few years ago, in the future impact zone beneath that oak, a screech owl perched on the cable strung between aging telephone poles—the torsos of trees from a thriving forest, stripped of their limbs and shackled by wires.

Last summer a family of foxes made a den up in the wooded part of Palfrey Hill at the end of our block. When the mother migrated to some other patch of suburban woods, one kit got left behind. For weeks its lonely yelp entered my dreams uninvited. Late one night Mishy and I looked out a front window and saw the orphan walking up our street in the direction of the woods. Mishy called out, "It's okay, little fox." A minute later it returned, stopped in the middle of the street, and looked up at us. Mishy talked to it again. In that moment, we were its community, though speaking an unfamiliar dialect.

Thirteen years ago the owner of the decaying carriage house that walls off the back of our yard installed screening along the eaves to keep squirrels from squeezing inside. For several springs we had seen litters pop their heads out from under the eaves and chase each other on the roof until they got skilled enough to leap onto the maple branches at the south end of the building. Once an osprey swooped down and knocked one of them out of the gutter, then flapped down to the lawn to grab the stunned infant in its talons. It then pumped its wings—to my eye, clumsily—and lifted off with its meal. In this ecosystem, though, the apex predators hark from a single species: *Homo sapiens*. They live in the three-story nests and other fabrications made possible by their cerebral cortexes, opposable thumbs, and tools.

On the north side of the carriage house, knotweed shoots up each spring in eight-foot imitations of bamboo. Its rhizomes tunnel stealthily down the slope, through our corner raspberry patch, and into the tomato cages on the top level of our terraced vegetable garden. Other plants join this invasion—verdolaga, spotted spurge, carpet weed, and common mullein.

Even in this semi-urban environment, wild critters are every-where. The osprey, the owl. Cardinals and foxes. Mice squeeze inside our house each winter for warmth. In the spring ants march in for water. Squirrels leap onto the bird feeder hanging over our back deck. A family of garter snakes set up home under the *Rosa rugosa* out front last summer. Moths plaster themselves on the garage door each September. About five years ago an "animal control" worker trapped fourteen raccoons who had taken up residence in the car-riage house. Geese honk overhead in formation and poop effort-lessly on the Oak Hill Golf Course. They know how to manifest their Daoist de, their innate power—flying in *V* formations, swim-ming in ponds, grazing, fluttering their wings in display behavior, and yes, dropping green-black-white turds with abundant abandon. Maybe we should see them as a koan, and not just for golfers. Usu-ally humans try to shoo them, drawing on our own de: shouting obscenities, throwing tennis balls, taking a run at them with golf carts.

Even if we reinhabit our local places and, like on the trail, pay attention to the wildness around us that is pooping on fairways, scurrying around dumpsters, and hoping for bread crumbs in city parks, wilderness still needs protection, especially from extractive industries that mine, drill, and clear-cut for short-term gain. We need to keep asking, what is the value of wilderness? What places are worth protecting? Jack Turner gives his answer:

> If the parks and wilderness areas must preserve anything, even at the cost of unpopularity, it must be this: the pos-sibility of contact with wild forms of being. This requires two things. First, we must preserve those other things as freely existing, self-organizing nations in their own right. Second, we must preserve true contact with them, simple,

unmediated contact, contact with our bodies, our senses, contact where what we experience is their presence.[127]

Perhaps the key is not simply such contact but places where wild beings, especially those high up the food chain, can flourish undisturbed. We can afford to let them be, for our adventurous spirits don't have to go on pilgrimage to the backcountry to make contact with wild forms of being. The two-foot snapping turtle lurking in one bend of the Charles between here and Waltham deserves respect. Neighborhood kids are wise to steer clear of the raccoons living in the abandoned house on Palfrey Hill. The yellow jackets that stung me the other day out by the garage were anything but domesticated.

This and much more is happening here in my place. I can notice it if I shut off the computer and head outside to experience what is transpiring around me. Clouds are passing overhead. The cardinals are feeding their chicks. Mildew is growing on the north side of the house. We can heal ourselves from nature-deficit disorder by getting out into the back yard or nearest park. We can pay attention to what's happening, and not simply through immediate sense experience but by recognizing, monitoring, and tracking things.

When Mishy and I went to the Canadian Rockies a decade ago, we found that a scenic overlook along the Icefields Parkway featured displays with maps and photos charting the recession of the glacier across the valley. It showed where the terminus of the glacier was in 1930 and in 1957 and in 1990. A vivid display of global warming—honest, stark, undeniable. The next year we went to Glacier National Park in the U.S. and were immediately struck by the lack of such displays, even at a park championing glaciers in its name. After noting the umpteenth spot where there could have been a display, we finally asked a ranger, "Why aren't there any displays mapping the recession of the glaciers like there are up in Banff and

Jasper? Is it because of some directive from the Interior Department under Bush?" "No, not really," she responded. To elaborate she said something like, "A lot of the visitors to the park come from Montana, Wyoming, and Colorado and work for oil and natural gas companies. While on vacation they don't really want to see displays that raise questions about their employers and imply that we should shift our consumption patterns in ways that could cost them their jobs."

Rising global temperatures are, of course, doing more than simply melting the rivers of ice in the Rockies. With the gradual warming of New England, robins have been wintering on Cape Cod. The Carolina chickadee is moving north, and its local cousins are seeking habitat in the Adirondacks and Ontario. Outside the window on the right side of my study is a thirty-foot hemlock, wedged between the corner of our house and our neighbors' garage. Its lower branches hide a leaf pile, and up high the sparrows congregate and dart to the feeder hanging above our back deck. Several summers ago their flitting drew my attention away from my laptop. I noticed that the tips of several branches were white, as if flocked in anticipation of Christmas. When I stepped out back later to harvest some zucchini blossoms, I saw that the white foam was spread across the lower half of the tree. Out loud I said, "Oh no." A few weeks earlier the *Boston Globe* had carried an article about the wooly adelgid and its devastation of hemlocks along the Atlantic coast. The bug's habitat had spread from Georgia, where, according to another article, poison ivy has been flourishing, with its vines getting thicker and the urushiol getting more toxic to human skin as temperatures rise. Here in our town, poison ivy is running amok beside the walkway along the Charles from Watertown Square to Moody Street in Waltham.

This, too, is part of my place, part of the nature—and wildness—in and around me.

TEN

True Home, True Pilgrimage

HONCHI —
"ORIGINAL
GROUND"

> Pilgrims are persons in motion—passing through terri-
> tories not their own—seeking something we might call
> completion, or perhaps the word clarity will do as well, a
> goal to which the spirit's compass points the way.
>
> —RICHARD R. NIEBUHR[128]

> We are all visitors to this time, this place.
> We are just passing through.
> Our purpose here is to observe, to learn, to grow,
> to love . . . and then
> we return home.
>
> —AUSTRALIAN ABORIGINAL PROVERB[129]

B ACK OFF THE TRAIL, the pilgrimage is not necessarily over. We are not stuck at home.

We can see our abode as our base camp, a place from which we go on additional pilgrimages. Fully emplaced in our bodies, houses, neighborhoods, communities, bioregions, we can construe pilgrimage in broader terms than circumambulation of Mount Kailash or backpacking trips in the White Mountains. Pilgrimage doesn't require places of divine revelation. It doesn't need to be about getting closer to higher beings or having peak experiences. When asked where we can find the sacred, Zen masters have told us to pick up our bowls, to look at the cypress tree in the garden, to hear a pebble hitting bamboo. Other mystics proclaim that God or the Great Spirit is all around us.

But can we open our minds, pay attention, and feel that presence? Being able to attune ourselves to the sanctity around us, or if you prefer, the beauty and wonder, may call for attention and *intention*: approaching each excursion beyond the threshold of our home as a pilgrimage, as a journey of openness and awe. Phil Cousineau writes, "With a deepening of focus, keen preparation, attention to the path below our feet, and respect for the destination at hand, it is possible to transform even the most ordinary trip into a sacred journey, a pilgrimage."[130]

With this mindset, we can stroll through the neighborhood, go for a walk in a nearby park, or simply step out into the garden as a pilgrimage. Whenever we depart, go somewhere, and return, we are on a journey, however brief. Unless our home itself is dangerous, we let go of security, just like when we head into the mountains. We take a risk every time we step out the front door and into the world. Things are less predictable. We may be surprised. We may encounter someone or something unexpected. We may find that a delayed bus or a sudden downpour interrupts our plans. As Jim Forest puts it, "Pilgrimage, in the sense of a religious journey along an unfamiliar path undertaken by foot, is by definition an extended interruption. Ordinary life, with all its routine actions and well-established schedules, is abandoned.... The familiar evaporates."[131] In this liminal state, we are open to surprise and interruption, and we greet them as opportunities to learn. As Forest puts it, "Pilgrimage is a school in which we attempt to see God's hand not only in what we hoped for but in what we didn't want to happen. It's the losing method of finding. ... The only plan you have is what path to follow, and even that doesn't work out as you imagined it would."[132]

Even when we follow this "losing method" by letting go of our expectations and attachments, we find things on our journey. We may not encounter the sacred or experience something worth labeling "epic," and the liminality may be tame and short-lived, but we have gone on a journey, and if we have gone with openness and paid attention, we'll see that we've returned with a boon. It may not be a vial of healing water, an epiphany, or deeper faith. At the very least, however, we've experienced something new. We may notice certain things for the first time, or see familiar things in a new light. We have woken up—at least a bit—to what is around us.

Perhaps the pilgrim's spirit is encapsulated in that expression from the tea ceremony: ichigo ichi'e, one moment, a singular encounter. Central to the art of tea and the art of living is this ability to bring openness and curiosity to each outing, to greet each never-to-be-repeated encounter as an opportunity to experience something new, to learn, to change, even if only slightly. To cultivate this we have to let go of the desire for certainty, for closure, for perfection. Formal pilgrimage provides a structure for this, a template that can be applied to all our outings, like today's quick trip to the store to get some onions and yams to grill out back.

In addition to micro-pilgrimages like these, we can also imagine macro-pilgrimages, which roam wider and last longer than a weekend on the Appalachian Trail or a two-week trip to Lourdes. They may be a stint in the military, four years in college, or decades of living far from where we grew up. In our youth we expand outward, wandering out of the house on infant legs, then venturing farther afield as an adolescent, seeking a grander vision of things, maybe in the mountains, or on the road in foreign countries. In the hero archetype that Joseph Campbell claimed is lodged in our collective unconscious, we venture far away to slay dragons or find a golden fleece. Not that we are all lucky enough to do this—most people in this world are too poor or too restricted to contemplate the luxury of grand journeys of exploration. (And not that the hero archetype, with the masculine triumphalism it implies to some, is the best paradigm for human growth.)

I went on such an extended pilgrimage—to Japan, California, and Washington State—lasting twenty-five years. Then I moved back East. It wasn't to my hometown of Litchfield but to Boston, several hours from aging parents, brother, sisters-in-law, nieces and nephews, and two great-nephews. Maybe it was time to let go of my quest for intense experiences. For me, the path now is less about meditating in Kyoto than fixing bowls of ice cream on warm brownies for Pop in what turned out to be the last year of his life.

I have also returned to mossy streams, crumbling stone walls, and forested hills. The scenery is not as majestic as the North Cascades, so on my pilgrimages out into nature I try to recognize the wild in its smaller forms and appreciate the beauty of smaller things, like the one dandelion growing in the strip between the sidewalk and the road out front.

It is here, in this region, that I choose to make my home-monastery for practice, to "settle down." It is more crowded than out west, and our work has us living in a semi-urban location, so recently my role model is less Han Shan up on Cold Mountain than Dao Yuanming, who back in the fifth century wrote,

> I built my hut within the world of men,
> But there is no noise of carriages and horses.
> You may ask how this is possible:
> When the heart is subdued, solitude comes.[133]

At times, though, it has felt like a sacrifice leaving the large-scale nature of the West Coast and returning to smaller-scale, more crowded New England. Paradoxically, though, it has been a sacrifice not only in the ordinary sense of the word but in the literal meaning: "making sacred." Whether going on a pilgrimage, backpacking, or coming off the road after being away for twenty-five years, sacrifices on the journey are a part of *making sacred*. Many pilgrims feel sanctified through the renunciation of their comfort zones and undergoing trials on the way to a place where a divinity has appeared. Once at that spot, the closer contact with the sacred may strengthen faith and make our life feel holy. Or the "making sacred" may take the form of sloughing off egocentricity and getting back in touch with the spark of the sacred within us, or (re)appropriating one's home, (re)inhabiting a place, and attuning oneself to the nature, the wildness, the beauty all around.

Rather than "the sacred," Buddhists might prefer wording like "buddha-nature": the awareness that resides in the nonduality between self and the world, the awareness of being embedded in nature, with the natural world as our true body. To quote Snyder again, "The point is to make intimate contact with the real world, real self. Sacred refers to that which helps take us out of our little selves into the whole mountains-and-rivers mandala universe."[134]

At this point in my life it is the mountains-and-rivers mandala universe all around me in New England, including its streets and buildings. I try to study and learn this region. I breathe it in, smell it, taste it, and pay attention to what's unfolding around me. I try to map it in myself and let it imprint itself on me, like what happened in my childhood with the woods down by the river in the valley across the street. As Martin Buber has written, "All real living is meeting,"[135] and the pilgrimage, the path, is not simply meeting other people and engaging difference, ambiguity, and conflict but meeting the nature around us with open eyes and sweating body. In this mode of learning on the path, education is not about what we know but who we become.

For those of us whose life pilgrimages have taken us to other countries, when we reinhabit our home place or inhabit a new place, we may feel translocal or omnilocal, a global citizen as much as an

American or a Japanese one. The koan here is how to be cosmopolitan while also inhabiting one's local place, with an understanding of its natural features, folklore, history, and politics. It's the challenge of retaining the pilgrim's sense of journey across a vast world while also lobbying the town council to ban fracking or listening to an angry neighbor ranting about dogs pooping in the park at the end of the block. It's the practice of balancing the grand vision, the big picture, with everyday detail, whether the bugs eating the basil in the window box or the flat tire on the way to a Little League game. Through this we find our niche, extending out from the kitchen to the planet as a whole. As Sharon Daloz Parks puts it, "To be at home is to have a place in the scheme of things—a place where we are comfortable; know that we belong; can be who we are; and can honor, protect, and create what we truly love. To be at home within one's self, place, community, and the cosmos is to feel whole and connected in a way that yields power and participation."[136]

Perhaps it is all part of a great journey, a master hike of sorts. In key respects, we can see our entire life is a pilgrimage. We are born in a place, journey for however long we are blessed to be alive, in search of something, dealing with this or that adversity along the way. The goal may be peace of mind, a loving family, rootedness in a place, or happiness in some other form. For some the goal comes at the end of our sojourning here, in the Elysian Fields, a paradise on high, the Great Beyond. We arrive in this world as pilgrims, and as pilgrims we depart. We are born naked, from a dark womb, and leave naked, wrapped in a shroud or our best outfit, placed in a box or fired into ashes, then returned to the subterranean belly of Mother Earth or poured into a "body" of water.

In ordinary pilgrimage, whether on the trail or to sacred sites, we look outside ourselves and travel to a distant place, maybe in foreign lands. We get away from our mundane concerns, hoping to find something powerful, reassuring, healing. We may seek to overcome our despair and shake off the feeling of being adrift in a surreal movie. We look to refresh ourselves, have a powerful experience, renew our faith. For many of us, these concerns span a lifetime. Christians might say that across a lifetime we travel from God and back to God. Some in East Asia might say the journey is from and then back to the Dao, the nameless, the mysterious female. Plotinus saw our life journey as a return to the "place from which we came." At the very least, we can live a life "on the path," ideally a path with heart, as Don Juan supposedly advocated to Carlos Castaneda.

This lifelong pilgrimage does not necessarily lead us back to where we started. Unlike Victor Turner's pilgrimage, we may not "reaggregate" into the social structure from which we departed. God knows that many homes and hometowns can be constrictive if not toxic; in those cases, after leaving, the wise approach is to never look back, or at least never go back.

But we must be careful, lest we look perpetually outside ourselves. For many of us, the true home we are seeking is not the hearth or the building in which we reside, or even a heaven on high, but the heart, or, as the Japanese would have it, our heart-mind (*kokoro*). You don't need to be in pristine wilderness, or in the Church of the Holy Sepulchre, at the Kaaba, or beneath the Kotel. Such power spots may help us let go of our self-centeredness and draw closer to the divine, but they may also deepen the rift between "me" standing here and the something sacred "over there." On the path I'm imagining, the truth and the true teacher are not outside us. Linji spoke of "being on the road but never having left home." What is this home that is there with us, inside us, each step of the way on the Camino in northern Spain or the Appalachian Trail in northern New Hampshire?

Usually we don't know. When we try to find this home, it slips away into the shadows. But we know it's there. It's our source, the wholeness from which we separated when we embraced the reflective consciousness that makes us human but leaves us alienated. We sense it in our depths and we long for it. Perhaps this is what Pico Iyer was getting at when he wrote that "every one of us carries around, inside, a certain, unnamed homesickness, a longing for a place we left and don't know how to find again."[137] For many Hindus, it's Brahman, a fundamental oneness. Some Buddhists see it as buddha-nature. For others, it's the soul, or perhaps a higher consciousness that we taste from time to time as something ancient, usually hiding just out of sight.

We may get swept with nostalgia for the times we felt this source or for a childhood when the woods were still enchanted and we could intuit the presence of spirits and elves. This may nudge us out onto the trail, or onto the road. But beware of quests for something in the past. As Linji told us, what we're seeking, the sacred destination, our true home, has been inside us all along. The sacred does not reside in the past—what we're looking for is right here, right now. Thich Nhat Hanh writes, "We are going home in every moment—we are practically going home in every moment to mother earth, to God, to the ultimate dimension, to our true nature of no birth, no death. That is our true home. We have never left our home."[138]

This seeking, on a pilgrimage across a lifetime, may be the key to living a meaningful life. At the very least it accords with what most of the world's religions have been getting at with their myths and practices. As Kerry Temple so eloquently puts it,

> Most of the world's religions look back to a lost and cherished age, a mythical, Edenic period—a time out of time—characterized by a more intimate union with God. The story of life on earth, then, is a story of a separation from God, of an estrangement, of a fallen race wandering in the desert, of a journey back to God, toward a reuniting, a reunion, a redemption. And what guides that return, that journey

back to the eternal are improbable and enigmatic moments of clarity—fleeting signs and flashing revelations, epiphanies, illuminations, *satori*. And faith. This ancient story, retold in culture after culture, is even more relevant today for a human race whose pursuit of material, temporal gods has led it out worthwhile but ultimately unfulfilling tangents. Or whose migration has left God and the promised land behind, frighteningly damaged. That reunion with nature's inherent spirit *is* the coming home.[139]

For the pilgrim on this journey, Einstein's teaching rings true: it is not that there are no mysteries left in the world but that the entire world is one great mystery. We are the restless spirits, the seekers with a lust for exploration, traveling light, with fear and trembling, reverence and awe, and an eight-ounce bottle of Pepto-Bismol. Our peripatetic journey may never end, even, I assume, beyond the grave.

But we walk on pilgrimage.

Each day—down the street, or on the trail . . . and across the planet, into the far reaches of our psyche.

Wandering, sensing, taking it all in.

So we saunter toward the Holy Land, till one day the sun shall shine more brightly than ever he has done, shall perchance shine into our minds and hearts, and light up our whole lives with a great awakening light, as warm and serene and golden as on a bankside in autumn.

—Henry David Thoreau[140]

Notes

1. Daisetz T. Suzuki, *Sengai: The Zen Master* (Greenwich, CT: New York Graphic Society, 1971), 25 (partially adapted).
2. John Stevens, *The Marathon Monks of Mount Hiei* (Boston: Shambhala, 1988), 67.
3. Victor Turner, *The Ritual Process: Structure and Anti-Structure* (New York: Routledge, 1995), 106-7.
4. Carol L. Winkelmann, "A Sakyadhita Pilgrimage: Frames, Images, and the Liminal Imagination," http://americanbuddhistwomen.com /carol-winkelmann.html: accessed June 13, 2017.
5. Phil Cousineau, *The Art of Pilgrimage: The Seeker's Guide to Making Travel Sacred* (San Francisco: Conari Press, 2000), xxix.
6. Huston Smith, foreword to *The Art of Pilgrimage*, by Cousineau, xi.
7. Diana L. Eck, *Darśan: Seeing the Diving Image in India*, 3rd ed. (New York: Columbia University Press, 1998), 3.
8. Ibid., 9.
9. All biblical quotations here come from *The New Oxford Annotated Bible*, 3rd. ed., ed. Michael D. Coogan (New York: Oxford University Press, 2007).
10. Gary Snyder, *The Practice of the Wild* (San Francisco: North Point Press, 1990), 94.
11. Ibid.
12. Ibid., 179.
13. This act mirrors the "great going forth" (Sanskrit *mahāpravrajyā*) of the Buddha, when he left his cushy life in his father's palace (and his wife and newborn son) and set out to seek answers to the existential questions that had been weighing on him.
14. Sōkō Morinaga, "My Struggle to Become a Zen Monk," in *Zen: Tradition & Transition*, ed. Kenneth Kraft (New York: Grove Press, 1988), 23.
15. Rupert Gethin, *The Foundations of Buddhism* (New York: Oxford University Press, 1998), 88.

16. Stephen Altschuler, *The Mindful Hiker: On the Trail to Find the Path* (Camarillo, CA: DeVorss & Company, 2004), 101.
17. In Chinese, *Wumenguan*, and in Japanese, *Mumonkan*.
18. Eishin Nishimura, *Unsui: Diary of Zen Monastic Life* (Honolulu: University of Hawaii Press, 1973), 4–6.
19. Quoted in Roderick Frazier Nash, *Wilderness and the American Mind*, 4th ed. (New Haven: Yale University Press, 2001), 5.
20. Daisetz T. Suzuki, *Zen and Japanese Culture* (Princeton: Princeton University Press, 1959), 23.
21. Ibid., 334.
22. Quoted in Fung Yu-lan, *A Short History of Chinese Philosophy* (New York: Free Press, 1966), 229.
23. Unlike these other poets, Gary Snyder did engage in traditional Zen training in Japan, and he does not consider himself a Beat poet.
24. Quoted in H. Byron Earhart, *Religion in the Japanese Experience: Sources and Interpretations* (Belmont CA: Wadsworth, 1974), 10; partially adapted here.
25. Snyder, *Practice of the Wild*, 5. Snyder comments that the Chinese (like the Japanese) became "removed enough from their mountains and rivers to aestheticize them" (22), and that although "the Chinese and Japanese have long given lip service to nature, only the early Daoists might have thought that wisdom could come of wildness" (6).
26. Ibid., 10.
27. Ibid., 12.
28. Gary Snyder, *A Place in Space: Ethics, Aesthetics, and Watersheds* (Washington, DC: Counterpoint, 1995), 168.
29. Ibid., 169.
30. Lambert Schmithausen, *Buddhism and Nature* (Tokyo: International Institute for Buddhist Studies, 1991), 16.
31. Peter Coates, *Nature: Western Attitudes since Ancient Times* (Berkeley: University of California Press, 2005), 58.
32. Quoted in Catherine L. Albanese, *Nature Religion in America: Algonkian Indians to the New Age* (Chicago: University of Chicago Press, 1990), 34.
33. Nash, *Wilderness*, 2.
34. Albanese, *Nature Religion in America*, 35.
35. Henry David Thoreau, *The Maine Woods* (New York: Thomas Y. Crowell, 1961), 81.
36. Ibid., 83–84.
37. Henry David Thoreau, "Walking," in *The Portable Thoreau*, ed. Jeffrey S. Cramer (New York: Penguin Books, 2012), 527.

38. Henry David Thoreau, *Walden and Civil Disobedience* (New York: Penguin Books, 1986), 366.

39. John Muir, *Our National Parks* (Boston: Houghton, Mifflin, 1901), 56.

40. Nash, *Wilderness*, xiv.

41. See Mark David Spence, *Dispossessing the Wilderness: Indian Removal and the Making of National Parks* (New York: Oxford University Press, 1999).

42. Snyder, *Practice of the Wild*, 88.

43. Rebecca Solnit, *Wanderlust: A History of Walking* (New York: Penguin Books, 2000), 5.

44. In an interview by Derrick Jensen, *Listening to the Land: Conversations about Nature, Culture, and Eros* (White River Junction, VT: Chelsea Green, 2004), 36

45. D.C. Lau, trans., *Tao Te Ching* (New York: Penguin Classics, 1964), 10.

46. Gerald May, *The Wisdom of Wilderness: Experiencing the Healing Power of Nature* (New York: HarperCollins, 2006), 62.

47. For a detailed discussion of this, see Steven Heine, *Zen Skin, Zen Marrow: Will the Real Zen Buddhism Please Stand Up?* (New York: Oxford University Press, 2008), 32.

48. Pico Iyer, foreword to *Traveling Souls: Contemporary Pilgrimage Stories*, ed. Brian Bouldrey (Berkeley: Whereabouts Press, 1999), vii.

49. Kōshō Uchiyama, *Opening the Hand of Thought: Approach to Zen* (New York: Arkana Books, 1993), 154.

50. Quoted in Albanese, *Nature Religion in America*, 90.

51. Quoted in Robert M. Hamma, *Earth's Echo: Sacred Encounters with Nature* (Notre Dame, IN: Sorin Books, 2002), 81.

52. Shunryu Suzuki, *Zen Mind, Beginner's Mind* (New York: Weatherhill, 2001), 62.

53. Kūkai's name literally means "Empty Sea." He is also known as Kōbō Daishi, which means "Great Teacher who Spreads the Dharma." He lived from 774 to 835.

54. Ian Reader, *Making Pilgrimages: Meaning and Practice in Shikoku* (Honolulu: University of Hawaii Press, 2005), 63.

55. Stevens, *Marathon Monks*, 63.

56. Thoreau, "Walking," 558.

57. John K. Nelson, *A Year in the Life of a Shinto Shrine* (Seattle: University of Washington Press, 1996), 34.

58. This poem is by the renowned Zen hermit Ryōkan (1758-1831). John Stevens, *Three Zen Masters* (New York: Kodansha International, 1993), 114-15.

59. Revata, "Revata's Farewell," the fourteenth set of verses in the *Theragatha*, Verses of Elder Monks, the eighth book of *Khuddaka Nikaya*, http://www.accesstoinsight.org/tipitaka/kn/thag/thag.14.01.than .html, accessed March 12, 2016.

60. Mark Coleman, *Awake in the Wild: Mindfulness in Nature as a Path of Self-Discovery* (Makawao, HI: Inner Ocean Publishing, 2006), xviii.

61. Max Moerman, *Localizing Paradise: Kumano Pilgrimage and the Religious Landscape of Premodern Japan* (Cambridge, MA: Harvard University Asia Center, 2006), 77.

62. Gary Snyder, "Walking the Great Ridge Omine on the Womb-Diamond Trail," in *The Sacred Mountains of Asia*, ed. John Einarsen (Boston: Shambhala, 1995), 72.

63. See Matthew Davis and Michael Farrell Scott, *Opening the Mountain: Circumambulating Mount Tamalpais, A Ritual Walk* (Emeryville, CA: Shoemaker & Hoard, 2006).

64. Kamo no Chōmei, "An Account of My Hut," in *Anthology of Japanese Literature*, trans. and ed. Donald Keene (New York: Evergreen Press: 1960), 206.

65. Thoreau, *Walden and Civil Disobedience*, 72.

66. Kamo no Chōmei, "Account of My Hut," 197.

67. William R. LaFleur, *The Karma of Words: Buddhism and the Literary Arts in Medieval Japan* (Berkeley: University of California Press, 1986), 79.

68. Kamo no Chōmei, "Account of My Hut," 211.

69. Flynn Johnson, *Journey to the Sacred Mountains: Awakening Your Soul in Nature* (Forres, Scotland: Findhorn Press, 2001), 32.

70. Ibid., 83.

71. Jack Turner, *The Abstract Wild* (Tucson: University of Arizona Press, 1996), 26.

72. Cousineau, *Art of Pilgrimage*, 70.

73. Amitabha in the west, represented by the color red; Amoghasiddi in the green north; Aksobhya in the blue east; Ratnasambhava in the golden south; and Vairocana in the white center.

74. Russell Johnson and Kerry Moran, *Tibet's Sacred Mountain: The Extraordinary Pilgrimage to Mount Kailas* (Rochester, VT: Park Street Press, 1989), 62–63.

75. John Muir, *Our National Parks* (1901), chapter 1, accessed February 19, 2018, https://vault.sierraclub.org/john_muir_exhibit/writings/ our_national_parks/chapter_1.aspx.

76. William Cronin, ed., *John Muir: Nature Writings* (New York: Library of America, 1997), 755.

77. Robert Alden Rubin, *On the Beaten Path: An Appalachian Pilgrimage*, 2nd ed. (Guilford, CT: Lyons Press, 2009), 21.

78. *Sankicca*, the eleventh set of verses in the *Theragatha*, Verses of Elder Monks, the eighth book of *Khuddaka Nikaya*, http://www.accesstoin sight.org/tipitaka/kn/thag/thag.11.01.than.html, accessed March 12, 2016.

79. James M. Hargett, *Stairway to Heaven: A Journey to the Summit of Mount Emei* (Albany: State University of New York Press, 2006), 10.

80. Ibid.

81. Ralph Waldo Emerson, "Nature," in *Ralph Waldo Emerson: Selected Prose and Poetry*, 2nd ed., ed. Reginald L. Cook (New York: Holt, Rinehard and Winston, 1969), 6.

82. Hargett, *Stairway to Heaven*, 9.

83. Arne Naess, "Mountains and Mythology," in *The Sacred Mountains of Asia*, ed. John Einarsen (Boston: Shambhala, 1995), 89.

84. Steven Heine, *Opening a Mountain: Kōans of the Zen Masters* (New York: Oxford University Press, 2002), 21.

85. Susan Naquin and Chün-fang Yü, introduction ("Pilgrimage in China") to *Pilgrims and Sacred Sites in China*, ed. Susan Naquin and Chün-fang Yü (Berkeley: University of California Press, 1992), 12.

86. Allan Grapard, "The Textualized Mountain—Enmountained Text: The Lotus Sutra in Kunisaki," in *The Lotus Sutra in Japanese Culture*, ed. George J. Tanabe Jr. and Willa Jane Tanabe (Honolulu: University of Hawaii Press, 1989), 173.

87. See Heine, *Opening a Mountain*, xiii.

88. Victoria Cass, *Dangerous Women: Warriors, Grannies, and Geishas of the Ming* (Lanham, MD: Rowman & Littlefield, 1999), 19; quoted in Heine, *Opening a Mountain*, 19.

89. Quoted from the *Theragatha* by Lily de Silva, "Early Buddhist Attitudes toward Nature," in *Dharma Rain: Sources of Buddhist Environmentalism*, ed. Stephanie Kaza and Kenneth Kraft (Boston: Shambhala, 2000), 101.

90. Dōgen Kigen, *Shōbōgenzō*, ed. Dōshū Ōkubo (Tokyo: Chikuma Shobō, 1971), 258.

91. Uchiyama, *Opening the Hand*, 153.

92. Thomas Cleary, trans., *The Book of Serenity* (New York: Lindisfarne Press, 1990), 390; quoted in Ruben L. F. Habito, "Mountains and Rivers and the Great Earth: Zen and Ecology," in *Buddhism and Ecol-*

ogy: The Interconnection of Dharma and Deeds, ed. Mary Evelyn Tucker and Duncan Ryūken Williams (Cambridge: Harvard University Press, 1997), 169.

93. Dōgen Kigen, *"Sokushin ze butsu,"* in *Shōbōgenzō* (Tokyo: Iwanami Bunko, 1939), 98; quoted in Habito, "Mountains and Rivers," 168.

94. This character is used to translate the Mahāyāna Buddhist technical term *śūnyāta*, usually rendered into English as "emptiness."

95. Thich Nhat Hanh, *Being Peace* (Berkeley: Parallax Press, 1990), 68–69.

96. John Muir, *My First Summer in the Sierra* (San Francisco: Sierra Club Books, 1988), 120.

97. David Barnhill, ed., *At Home on the Earth: Becoming Native to Our Place* (Berkeley: University of California Press, 1999), 5.

98. Dōgen Kigen, *Sansuikyō*, trans. Carl Bielefeldt, http://global.sotozen-net.or.jp/pdf/dharma-eye/hogen09/hogen09_07.htm, accessed February 11, 2018; partially adapted here.

99. Quoted in Joan Halifax, "The Third Body: Buddhism, Shamanism, and Deep Ecology," in *Dharma Gaia: A Harvest of Essays in Buddhism and Ecology*, ed. Allan Hunt Badiner (Berkeley: Parallax Press, 1990), 24.

100. Linnie Marsh Wolfe, ed., *John of the Mountains: The Unpublished Journals of John Muir* (Madison: University of Wisconsin Press, 1938; republished 1979), 439.

101. Jack Turner, *Abstract Wild*, 25.

102. Shin'ichi Hisamatsu, *Zen and the Fine Arts*, trans. Gishin Tokiwa (New York: Kodansha International, 1982). Not all art historians accept these seven characteristics as most descriptive of Zen art or agree with Hisamatsu's claim that only the awakened can fully understand Zen art, but his list is useful for our purposes here.

103. Shin'ichi Hisamatsu, *Critical Sermons of the Zen Tradition: Hisamatsu's Talks on Linji*, trans. and ed. Christopher Ives and Gishin Tokiwa (Honolulu: University of Hawaii Press, 2002), 32.

104. Hisamatsu, *Zen and the Fine Arts*, 58.

105. Ibid.

106. Ibid.

107. Steve Odin, "The Japanese Concept of Nature in Relation to the Environmental Ethics and Conservation Aesthetics of Aldo Leopold," in Tucker and Williams, eds., *Buddhism and Ecology*, 99.

108. Koh Masuda, ed., *Kenkyūsha's New Japanese-English Dictionary*, 4th ed. (Tokyo: Kenkyusha, 1974), 1,937.

109. Alan Campbell and David S. Noble, eds., *Japan: An Illustrated Encyclopedia* (Tokyo: Kodansha, 1993), 1,289.

110. Simon James, *Zen Buddhism and Environmental Ethics* (Burlington, VT: Ashgate Publishing Company, 2004), 73.

111. Sōtaku Jakuan, "The Zen Tea Record," in *Wind in the Pines: Classic Writings of the Way of Tea as a Buddhist Path*, trans. and ed. Dennis Hirota (Fremont, CA: Asian Humanities Press, 1995), 267 and 265.

112. Aldo Leopold, *A Sand County Almanac* (New York: Oxford University Press, 1965), 224-25.

113. Lizzie Bourne died on a cold, windy night without shelter near the summit of Mt. Washington after having tried to climb it that day with her father and sister. Nicholas Howe, *Not without Peril: 150 Years of Misadventure on the Presidential Range of New Hampshire* (Boston: Appalachian Mountain Club, 2001), 18-23.

114. Suzuki, *Zen and Japanese Culture*, 281.

115. Chapter 19 in the *Daodejing* includes the line, "Exhibit the unadorned and embrace the uncarved block."

116. Snyder, *Practice of the Wild*, 23-24.

117. Ibid., 179-80.

118. T. S. Eliot, *Four Quartets* (New York: Harcourt, Brace, and Company, 1943), 39.

119. Cousineau, *Art of Pilgrimage*, xiv.

120. Snyder, *Practice of the Wild*, 94.

121. Michael Pollan, *Second Nature: A Gardener's Education* (New York: Dell Publishers, 1991), 188.

122. Snyder, *A Place in Space*, 246-47.

123. Ibid., 190.

124. In this regard, all of us in eastern Massachusetts are indebted to William Cronon for *Changes in the Land*, and to John Hansen Mitchell for *Ceremonial Time, Walking towards Walden*, and *The Paradise of All These Parts*.

125. Wendy Johnson, *Gardening at the Dragon's Gate: At Work in the Wild and Cultivated World* (New York: Bantam Books, 2008), xv.

126. Ibid., 8.

127. Jack Turner, *Teewinot: Climbing and Contemplating the Teton Range* (New York: St. Martin's Press, 2000), 239.

128. Richard R. Niebuhr, "Pioneers and Pilgrims," *Parabola* IX, no. 3 (Fall 1984), 7.

129. Sheryl A. Kujawa-Holbrook, *Pilgrimage—the Sacred Art: Journey to the Center of the Heart* (Woodstock, VT: SkyLight Paths, 2013), 135.

130. Cousineau, *Art of Pilgrimage*, xxiii.

131. Jim Forest, *The Road to Emmaus: Pilgrimage as a Way of Life* (Maryknoll, NY: Orbis Books, 2007), 133-34.

132. Ibid., 135.

133. Cited in Zhang Longxi, *The Tao and the Logos: Literary Hermeneutics, East and West* (Durham, NC: Duke University Press, 1992), 124; cited and modified by Heine, *Zen Skin, Zen Marrow*, 51.

134. Snyder, *Practice of the Wild*, 94.

135. Martin Buber, *I and Thou*, 2nd ed., trans. Ronald Gregor Smith (New York: Charles Scribner's Sons, 1958), 11.

136. Sharon Daloz Parks, *Big Questions, Worthy Dreams: Mentoring Young Adults in Their Search for Meaning, Purpose, and Faith* (San Francisco: Jossey-Bass, 2000), 34; quoted in Kujawa-Holbrook, *Pilgrimage*, 152.

137. Iyer, foreword, xi.

138. Thich Nhat Hanh, *Essential Writings*, ed. Sister Annabel Laity (Maryknoll, NY: Orbis Books, 2001), 122-23; quoted in Kujawa-Holbrook, *Pilgrimage*, 164.

139. Kerry Temple, *Back to Earth: A Backpacker's Journey into Self and Soul* (Lanham MD: Rowman & Littlefield, 2005), 44.

140. Thoreau, "Walking," 589.

Bibliography

Albanese, Catherine L. *Nature Religion in America: Algonkian Indians to the New Age.* Chicago: University of Chicago Press, 1990.

Altschuler, Stephen. *The Mindful Hiker: On the Trail to Find the Path.* Camarillo, CA: DeVorss & Company, 2004.

Barnhill, David, ed. *At Home on the Earth: Becoming Native to Our Place.* Berkeley: University of California Press, 1999.

Campbell, Alan, and David S. Noble, eds. *Japan: An Illustrated Encyclopedia.* Tokyo: Kodansha, 1993.

Cass, Victoria. *Dangerous Women: Warriors, Grannies, and Geishas of the Ming.* Lanham, MD: Rowan & Littlefield, 1999.

Coates, Peter. *Nature: Western Attitudes since Ancient Times.* Berkeley: University of California Press, 2005.

Coleman, Mark. *Awake in the Wild: Mindfulness in Nature as a Path of Self-Discovery.* Makawao, HI: Inner Ocean Publishing, 2006.

Coogan, Michael D., ed. *The New Oxford Annotated Bible.* 3rd ed. New York: Oxford University Press, 2007.

Cousineau, Phil. *The Art of Pilgrimage: The Seeker's Guide to Making Travel Sacred.* San Francisco: Conari Press, 2000.

Cleary, Thomas, trans. *The Book of Serenity.* New York: Lindisfarne Press, 1990.

Cronon, William. *Changes in the Land: Indians, Colonists, and the Ecology of New England.* New York: Hill & Wang, 2003.

Davis, Matthew, and Michael Farrell Scott, *Opening the Mountain: Circumambulating Mount Tamalpais, A Ritual Walk.* Emeryville, CA: Shoemaker & Hoard, 2006.

de Silva, Lily. "Early Buddhist Attitudes toward Nature." In *Dharma Rain: Sources of Buddhist Environmentalism*, edited by Stephanie Kaza and Kenneth Kraft. Boston: Shambhala, 2000.

Dōgen Kigen. *Sansuikyō*, trans. Carl Bielefeldt, https://web.stanford.edu/group/scbs/sztp3/translations/shobogenzo/translations/sansuikyo/sansuikyo.html; accessed March 20, 2016.

——. *Shōbōgenzō*, ed. Dōshū Ōkubo. Tokyo: Chikuma Shobō, 1971.

——. *"Sokushin ze butsu."* In *Shōbōgenzō*. Tokyo: Iwanami Bunko, 1939.

Earhart, H. Byron. *Religion in the Japanese Experience: Sources and Inter-pretations*. Belmont, CA: Wadsworth, 1974.

Eck, Diana L. *Darśan: Seeing the Divine Image in India*. 3rd ed. New York: Columbia University Press, 1998.

Emerson, Ralph Waldo. "Nature." In *Ralph Waldo Emerson: Selected Prose and Poetry*, 2nd ed., edited by Reginald L. Cook. New York: Holt, Rine-hard and Winston, 1969.

Forest, Jim. *The Road to Emmaus: Pilgrimage as a Way of Life*. Maryknoll, NY: Orbis Books, 2007.

Fung Yu-lan. *A Short History of Chinese Philosophy*. New York: Free Press, 1966.

Gethin, Rupert. *The Foundations of Buddhism*. New York: Oxford University Press, 1998.

Grapard, Allan. "The Textualized Mountain—Enmountained Text: The Lotus Sutra in Kunisaki." In *The Lotus Sutra in Japanese Culture*, edited by George J. Tanabe Jr. and Willa Jane Tanabe. Honolulu: University of Hawaii Press, 1989.

Habito, Ruben L. F. "Mountains and Rivers and the Great Earth: Zen and Ecology." In *Buddhism and Ecology: The Interconnection of Dharma and Deeds*, edited by Mary Evelyn Tucker and Duncan Ryūken Williams. Cambridge: Harvard University Press, 1997.

Halifax, Joan. "The Third Body: Buddhism, Shamanism, and Deep Ecol-ogy." In *Dharma Gaia: A Harvest of Essays in Buddhism and Ecology*, edited by Allan Hunt Badiner. Berkeley: Parallax Press, 1990.

Hamma, Robert M. *Earth's Echo: Sacred Encounters with Nature*. Notre Dame, IN: Sorin Books, 2002.

Hargett, James M. *Stairway to Heaven: A Journey to the Summit of Mount Emei*. Albany: State University of New York Press, 2006.

Heine, Steven. *Opening a Mountain: Kōans of the Zen Masters*. New York: Oxford University Press, 2002.

——. *Zen Skin, Zen Marrow: Will the Real Zen Buddhism Please Stand Up?* New York: Oxford University Press, 2008.

Hisamatsu, Shin'ichi. *Critical Sermons of the Zen Tradition: Hisamatsu's Talks on Linji*. Translated and edited by Christopher Ives and Gishin Tokiwa. Honolulu: University of Hawaii Press, 2002.

——. *Zen and the Fine Arts*. Translated by Gishin Tokiwa. New York: Kodansha International, 1982.

Howe, Nicholas. *Not without Peril: 150 Years of Misadventure on the Presidential Range of New Hampshire.* Boston: Appalachian Mountain Club, 2001.

Iyer, Pico. Foreword to *Traveling Souls: Contemporary Pilgrimage Stories.* Edited by Brian Bouldrey. Berkeley: Whereabouts Press, 1999.

Jakuan, Sōtaku. "The Zen Tea Record." In *Wind in the Pines: Classic Writings of the Way of Tea as a Buddhist Path,* translated and edited by Dennis Hirota. Fremont, CA: Asian Humanities Press, 1995.

James, Simon. *Zen Buddhism and Environmental Ethics.* Burlington, VT: Ashgate Publishing Company, 2004.

Jensen, Derrick. *Listening to the Land: Conversations about Nature, Culture, and Eros.* White River Junction, VT: Chelsea Green, 2004.

Johnson, Flynn. *Journey to the Sacred Mountains: Awakening Your Soul in Nature.* Forres, Scotland: Findhorn Press, 2001.

Johnson, Russell, and Kerry Moran. *Tibet's Sacred Mountain: The Extraordinary Pilgrimage to Mount Kailas.* Rochester, VT: Park Street Press, 1989.

Johnson, Wendy. *Gardening at the Dragon's Gate: At Work in the Wild and Cultivated World.* New York: Bantam Books, 2008.

Kamo no Chōmei. "An Account of My Hut." In *Anthology of Japanese Literature,* translated and edited by Donald Keene. New York: Evergreen Press: 1960.

Kujawa-Holbrook, Sheryl A. *Pilgrimage—the Sacred Art: Journey to the Center of the Heart.* Woodstock, VT: SkyLight Paths, 2013.

LaFleur, William R. *The Karma of Words: Buddhism and the Literary Arts in Medieval Japan.* Berkeley: University of California Press, 1986.

Lau, D.C., trans. *Tao Te Ching.* New York: Penguin Classics, 1964.

Leopold, Aldo. *A Sand County Almanac.* New York: Oxford University Press, 1965.

Masuda, Koh, ed. *Kenkyūsha's New Japanese-English Dictionary.* 4th ed. Tokyo: Kenkyusha, 1974.

May, Gerald. *The Wisdom of Wilderness: Experiencing the Healing Power of Nature.* New York: HarperCollins, 2006.

Mitchell, John Hansen. *Ceremonial Time: Fifteen Thousand Years on One Square Mile.* Cambridge, MA: Perseus Books, 1984.

———. *The Paradise of All These Parts: A Natural History of Boston.* Boston: Beacon Press, 2008.

———. *Walking towards Walden: A Pilgrimage in Search of Place.* Cambridge, MA: Perseus Books, 1997.

Moerman, Max. *Localizing Paradise: Kumano Pilgrimage and the Religious Landscape of Premodern Japan*. Cambridge, MA: Harvard University Asia Center, 2006.

Morinaga, Sōkō. "My Struggle to Become a Zen Monk." In *Zen: Tradition & Transition*, edited by Kenneth Kraft. New York: Grove Press, 1988.

Muir, John. *My First Summer in the Sierra*. San Francisco: Sierra Club Books, 1988.

———. *Our National Parks*. Boston: Houghton, Mifflin, 1901.

Naess, Arne. "Mountains and Mythology." In *The Sacred Mountains of Asia*, edited by John Einarsen. Boston: Shambhala, 1995.

Naquin, Susan, and Chün-fang Yü. "Introduction: Pilgrimage in China." In *Pilgrims and Sacred Sites in China*, edited by Susan Naquin and Chün-fang Yü. Berkeley: University of California Press, 1992.

Nash, Roderick Frazier. *Wilderness and the American Mind*. 4th ed. New Haven: Yale University Press, 2001.

Nelson, John K. *A Year in the Life of a Shinto Shrine*. Seattle: University of Washington Press, 1996.

Nhat Hanh, Thich. *Being Peace*. Berkeley: Parallax Press, 1990.

———. *Essential Writings*. Edited by Sister Annabel Laity. Maryknoll, NY: Orbis Books, 2001.

Niebuhr, Richard R. "Pioneers and Pilgrims." *Parabola* IX, no. 3 (Fall 1984).

Nishimura, Eishin. *Unsui: Diary of Zen Monastic Life*. Honolulu: University of Hawaii Press, 1973.

Odin, Steve. "The Japanese Concept of Nature in Relation to the Environmental Ethics and Conservation Aesthetics of Aldo Leopold." In *Buddhism and Ecology: The Interconnection of Dharma and Deeds*, edited by Mary Evelyn Tucker and Duncan Ryūken Williams. Cambridge: Harvard University Press, 1997.

Parks, Sharon Daloz. *Big Questions, Worthy Dreams: Mentoring Young Adults in Their Search for Meaning, Purpose, and Faith*. San Francisco: Jossey-Bass, 2000.

Pollan, Michael. *Second Nature: A Gardener's Education*. New York: Dell Publishers, 1991.

Reader, Ian. *Making Pilgrimages: Meaning and Practice in Shikoku*. Honolulu: University of Hawaii Press, 2005.

Revata. "Revata's Farewell." http://www.accesstoinsight.org/tipitaka/kn/thag/thag.14.01.than.html; accessed March 12, 2016.

Rubin, Robert Alden. *On the Beaten Path: An Appalachian Pilgrimage*. 2nd ed. Guilford, CT: Lyons Press, 2009.

Sankicca. http://www.accesstoinsight.org/tipitaka/kn/thag/thag.11.01
.than.html; accessed March 12, 2016.

Schmithausen, Lambert. *Buddhism and Nature*. Tokyo: International
Institute for Buddhist Studies, 1991.

Smith, Huston. Introduction to *The Art of Pilgrimage: The Seeker's Guide to
Making Travel Sacred*, by Phil Cousineau. San Francisco: Conari Press,
2000.

Snyder, Gary. *A Place in Space: Ethics, Aesthetics, and Watersheds*. Washington, DC: Counterpoint, 1995.

——. *The Practice of the Wild*. San Francisco: North Point Press, 1990.

——. "Walking the Great Ridge Omine on the Womb-Diamond Trail." In
The Sacred Mountains of Asia, edited by John Einarsen. Boston: Shambhala, 1995.

Solnit, Rebecca. *Wanderlust: A History of Walking*. New York: Penguin
Books, 2000.

Spence, Mark David. *Dispossessing the Wilderness: Indian Removal and the
Making of National Parks*. New York: Oxford University Press, 1999.

Stevens, John. *The Marathon Monks of Mount Hiei*. Boston: Shambhala,
1988.

——. *Three Zen Masters*. New York: Kodansha International, 1993.

Suzuki, Daisetz T. *Sengai: The Zen Master*. Greenwich, CT: New York
Graphic Society, 1971.

——. *Zen and Japanese Culture*. Princeton: Princeton University Press,
1959.

Suzuki, Shunryu. *Zen Mind, Beginner's Mind*. New York: Weatherhill,
2001.

Temple, Kerry. *Back to Earth: A Backpacker's Journey into Self and Soul*.
Lanham, MD: Rowman & Littlefield, 2005.

Thoreau, Henry David. *The Maine Woods*. New York: Thomas Y. Crowell,
1961.

——. *Walden and Civil Disobedience*. New York: Penguin Books, 1986.

——. "Walking." In *The Portable Thoreau*, edited by Jeffrey S. Cramer.
New York: Penguin Books, 2012.

Turner, Jack. *The Abstract Wild*. Tucson: University of Arizona Press, 1996.

——. *Teewinot: Climbing and Contemplating the Teton Range*. New York: St.
Martin's Press, 2000.

Turner, Victor. *The Ritual Process: Structure and Anti-Structure*. New York:
Routledge, 1995.

Uchiyama, Kōshō. *Opening the Hand of Thought: Approach to Zen*. New
York: Arkana Books, 1993.

Winkelmann, Carol L. "A Sakyadhita Pilgrimage: Frames, Images, and the Liminal Imagination." http://americanbuddhistwomen.com /carol-winkelmann.html; accessed June 13, 2017.

Zhang Longxi. *The Tao and the Logos: Literary Hermeneutics, East and West.* Durham, NC: Duke University Press, 1992.

Index

when in nature, 96, 115, 130, 136
See also gūjin
awakened beings, 64. See also
   specific beings
awakening, 25, 76
   of Buddha, 94, 121
   and understanding Zen art,
     156n102
   See also enlightenment;
     transformation

B
Barnhill, David, 101
Bashō, 87, 96
beauty, 104, 107-9, 113. *See also*
   aesthetics
Bernadette of Lourdes, 8, 94
Berry, Thomas, 37
Bible, 12, 25, 61, 82, 117-18
Bodhi Tree, 8, 94, 121
bodhisattvas, 9, 64, 65, 85, 114
body
   attention to, 101
   pilgrimages and the, 12, 13
   practice of throwing away the, 64
   religion and the, 12
bonding through acts of generosity, 144-45
bonfire rituals, 1, 4
born again, getting, 55
Bourne, Lizzie, 112, 157n113
Bradford, William, 32
breathing, 39-40, 59
Buber, Martin, 143
Buddha (Siddhartha Gautama), 9,
   58-59, 83, 151n13
   body of, 48
   enlightenment/awakening, 64,
     94, 121

sitting under tree, 94 (*see also*
   Bodhi Tree)
   Zen monasteries and, 48
buddha-nature, 143, 146
buddhas, 63, 64
Buddhism
   Japanese, 3, 4
   Mahāyāna, 114-16
   mandalas and, 63-64, 75, 86
   Tibetan, 63, 85
   See also specific topics
Buddhist pilgrimages, 9, 75
Bunyan, John, 54

C
Campbell, Joseph, 141
campfires, 4, 70-73, 111. *See also*
   fire
campsites, 68, 124
   setting up, 66
Castaneda, Carlos, 145
cats, 45. *See also* cougars; Rusty
   (cat)
cell phone, 20-21
Chinese, 41
   mountains and the, 44, 83-87
Chinese mountains, 82, 85,
   152n25
Chōmei, Kamo no, 67-68
Christianity, 12
circumabulation, 75-76
climate change, 137
Clinton Trail, Mount, 62, 66
Coates, Peter, 32
Coleman, Mark, 63
Coleridge, Samuel Taylor, 82
communion, 55
   with nature, 101
   See also *communitas*
communitas, 10, 114

consciousness, shifts in, 100–101

conservation, 111–12. *See also* environmentalism and environmental ethic

cooking, 124. *See also* tea ceremonies

cooking gear, 18. *See also* hiking gear

cougars, 44, 45, 47

Cousineau, Phil, 10, 140

Crawford, Ethan, 120

Crawford Notch, 44, 118–20

Crawford Path, 21, 77, 84, 93, 99, 103, 104, 113–14, 127

Cronon, William, 157n124

curiosity, sustained, 10

Curtis, William, 104

D

daily life, pilgrimages taking the seeker away from, 9

Daoism, 43, 104, 116–17

darshan, 11

datsuzoku, 51

de (virtue), 116, 135

de Angulo, Jaime, 102

death, imagery of, 54–55

defilements, 113

Diamond Realm and Womb Realm, 63, 64, 86

divine, (re)connection with the, 11–12, 14

Dōgen, 3, 38–40, 96, 98

on *gūjin*, 38–39, 53

and the mind, 93, 96

on mountains, 88, 93, 101–2

on mountains constantly walking, 40, 130

on waters, 88

Dry River, 17, 66, 116

hiking along, 37–38, 41, 47, 60, 69, 127 (*see also* Dry River Trail; Dry River Valley)

Dry River Cutoff, 66, 79, 80

Dry River drainage, 20, 27, 57

Dry River Trail, 26, 44, 53, 120. *See also* Dry River

Dry River Valley, 23, 35, 125

E

earth, element of, 42–43

East-West binary, 28–29

eating, mindful, 68–69

Eck, Diana, 11

ecstasy, 13–14

ego, 89, 90, 112. *See also* self: forgetting the

Eightfold Path, 125–26

Einstein, Albert, 147

electronics, 20–21

elements, four, 42–43, 76

Eliot, T. S., 119

embodiment, 13

Emerson, Ralph Waldo, 53, 82–83, 94

emptiness, 95, 116

as form, 97 (*see also* Formless Self)

empty-sky mind, 95–96. *See also* mind: emptying one's

enlightenment

nature and, 70

See also awakening

Enryakuji, 3–5, 7

entering, 24–27

liminality, 9, 10

moment of, 26

mountains, 82, 86

environmentalism and environ-

pilgrimage stripping us of "back in the world," 55

See also self

impermanence, 54, 66–67, 99, 116

intention, 140

Isaac, 9

Iyer, Pico, 51, 146

J

jaku (tranquility), 110, 113

James, Simon, 109

Japan, 6–7, 30–31, 63, 65, 106, 107, 125

  Gary Snyder on, 34–35

  gender roles in, 30, 31

  Ives in, 1–7

  mountains in, 30, 85, 87

  nature and, 28–32, 35

  pilgrimages to, 9

  pilgrims in, 9, 76–77

  temples in, 3, 86

  tourism in, 5–7

  See also specific topics

Japanese religions, 3, 6, 29–31. *See also specific religions*

Jefferson, Thomas, 108

Jerusalem, pilgrims to, 100

Jesus Christ, 12, 25, 74

jinen, 105

Johnson, Flynn, 71

Johnson, Wendy, 132

joy, 13–14

Julian of Norwich, 94

K

Kailish, Mount, 13, 75, 84, 85, 139

Kanmu, Emperor, 3

Kannon, 9

kanso (simplicity), 104–5

Kerouac, Jack, 15, 29, 31

kinhin (walking meditation), 38

kleshas, 113

Ko Hung. *See* Ge Hong

kokō ("lofty dryness"), 105

Kūkai (Kōbō Daishi), 54, 75, 87, 153n53

L

Lafayette, Mount, 43–44

"leave no trace," 53, 112, 125

  principles of, 115

Leopold, Aldo, 59, 101, 110

Lesser, Mishy, 21

letting go, 51–56, 140–41. *See also* mind: emptying one's

liminal moments, 14

liminal state, 10, 13, 55, 140, 141

liminality and the liminal realm, 9–10

Linji Yixuan, 105, 145, 146

Linnaeus, Carl, 118

listening, 38

"live deliberately," 38, 123

loop, walking/hiking in a, 75, 77

love, 71

  sensual, 11–12

  types of, 11–12, 28, 30

  See also nature: "love of nature"

M

MacKaye, Benton, 80

macro-pilgrimages, 142

Mahakashyapa, 87–88

Mahāyāna Buddhism, 114–16

mandala universe, mountains-and-rivers, 14, 143

mandalas, 4

  buddhas and, 63, 64

  Buddhism and, 63–64, 75, 86

  circles and, 76

Murdoch, Iris, 101
mushin (no mind), 95–96, 105

N
Naess, Arne, 83
nature
  attention when in, 96, 115, 130,
    136
  being, 16, 98
  connection to, 128–30, 135–36
  "conquest of nature," 28
  Japan and, 28–32, 35
  "love of nature," 28, 30, 35, 103
  participating in vs. simply
    observing, 63
  terminology, 29–31
  wild vs. tamed/stylized, 30–32
nature-deficit disorder, 136
Nelson, John, 57
Nhat Hanh, Thich, 97, 146
Nichiren, 3
Niebuhr, Richard R., 139
Nishimura, Eishin, 26
niwa zume, 26
nonattachment, 51. See also
  letting go
nonduality, 96–97, 101, 143
Norinaga, Motoori, 30

O
Oda, Nobunaga, 4
openness, 10
Ormsbee, Allan, 104
Otto, Rudolf, 61, 83

P
packing ritual, 21–25. *See also*
  hiking gear
pain, 13
  acceptance of, 12

value of, 48–49
pāramitās (perfections), 114–16
Parks, Sharon Daloz, 144
patience, perfected, 115
peregrination, 8
perfections of Mahāyāna Buddhism, 114–16
Pierce, Mount (New Hampshire),
  66, 81, 84, 90, 99, 104, 105,
  108, 116
pilgrimage(s), 8
  (living) life as a, vii, 144
  aftereffects of, 121–23
  approaching each excursion as
    a, 139–40
  benefits gained from, 11, 12
  characteristics, 13
  definitions, 8, 140
  essence of, 10
  etymology of the word, 8
  goals/aims of and motivations
    for, 8, 11, 130
  heading home and resuming
    ordinary life after, 121–25
  hiking compared with, vii, 7, 13,
    14, 54
  how to transform any trip into
    a, 140
  lifelong, 16, 143–47
  micro- and macro-, 142
  in the myths and practices of
    religions, 146–47 (*see also* reli-
    gions: pilgrimages and)
  nature of, 8–13, 55, 58, 140,
    144–45
  to other countries, 143–44
  psychological benefits, 121–23
  what makes a hike a, vii
  See also specific topics
pilgrims, 10, 55

About the Author

CHRISTOPHER IVES is a professor of religious studies at Stonehill College. In his teaching and writing he focuses on ethics in Zen Buddhism and Buddhist approaches to nature and environmental issues. His publications include *Imperial-Way Zen: Ichikawa Hakugen's Critique and Lingering Questions for Buddhist Ethics*; *Zen Awakening and Society*; *Divine Emptiness and Historical Fullness*; a translation (with Abe Masao) of Nishida Kitarō's *An Inquiry into the Good*; and a translation (with Gishin Tokiwa) of Hisamatsu Shin'ichi's *Critical Sermons of the Zen Tradition*. He is on the editorial board of the *Journal of Buddhist Ethics* and is serving as cochair of the Buddhist Critical-Constructive Reflection Group and on the steering committee of the Religion and Ecology Group of the American Academy of Religion.

What to Read Next
from Wisdom Publications

....

DEEP DOWN THINGS
The Earth in Celebration and Dismay
Lin Jensen

"Lin Jensen is the clearest voice in Buddhism. Highly and urgently recommended."—Karen Maezen Miller, author of *Hand Wash Cold*

LANDSCAPES OF WONDER
Discovering Buddhist Dhamma in the World Around Us
Bhikkhu Nyanasobhano
Foreword by Bhikkhu Bodhi

"One of the most melodious new voices in Western Buddhism to come along in some while."—Amazon.com

ZEN MEDITATION IN PLAIN ENGLISH
John Daishin Buksbazen
Foreword by Peter Matthiessen

"A fine introduction to Zen meditation practice, grounded in tradition yet adapted to contemporary life."—*Publishers Weekly*

ZEN MASTER RAVEN
The Teachings of a Wise Old Bird
Robert Aitken
Foreword by Nelson Foster

"A new koan anthology that reflects the distinct flavor of American Zen Buddhist practice. This is a beautiful and worthy final teaching from Aitken."—*Publishers Weekly*

About Wisdom Publications

Wisdom Publications is the leading publisher of classic and contemporary Buddhist books and practical works on mindfulness. To learn more about us or to explore our other books, please visit our website at wisdompubs.org or contact us at the address below.

Wisdom Publications
199 Elm Street
Somerville, MA 02144 USA

We are a 501(c)(3) organization, and donations in support of our mission are tax deductible.

Wisdom Publications is affiliated with the Foundation for the Preservation of the Mahayana Tradition (FPMT).